MW01259609

Ultimate Big Game Adventures

WILD HUNTS ACROSS NORTH AMERICA

BY JIM SHOCKEY

For Louise,

Cold means nothing.
Wind blows and rain falls;
the next mountain is higher than the last
and the next river deeper;
another impossible mile to go ...
all nothing by compare
to enduring the time away from you.

We have shared the moon.

Book design: White Dog Design Co. • Photo credits: Jim Shockey.

Published by: Folkart Interiors, Ltd., #340, 185-911 Yates St., Victoria, British Columbia, Canada V8V 4Y9.

To order Jim Shockey publications or videos, please visit www.JimShockey.com

ISBN 0-97328080-8

10 9 8 7 6 5 4 3 2 1

Printed in the United States of America

ISBN 0-97328080-8

9 780973 280807

ACKNOWLEDGMENTS

First the excuse; about 20 years ago I started on the trail that was to lead to this book, 20 years of too many things to remember and too many people to thank. Forgive me if you should be here but are not, it isn't that you weren't intended to be here, it's simply that my hard drive is full. At my age, when I add a new memory an old one gets deleted. Hopefully the handful of vitamins that my wife feeds me every night will slow the antiquating process. But in the meantime, a word of advice to any young writers who intend to start writing now, but not complete a first book until 20 years from now … take notes!

Mom and Dad, thanks. Without your understanding and unconditional love for this restless youth, I'd probably be planning my next breakout instead of my next hunt.

Louise, what can I write about your unwavering support that I haven't already penned? No, on second thought, that's not a good question. My editor says that I only have 500 words here; it would take another book, 1,000 times the size of this one, to even begin to thank you for everything that you've done to make this book a reality. I promise to make the last two decades up to you … as soon as I peek over the next hill …

While we're talking family, my two incredible children need to be acknowledged for their part in the making of this book. Theirs wasn't a father who made every soccer game or field hockey match, and yet they have never held back their love. Branlin and Eva, thanks for not finding me guilty … even if I am.

Guy Shockey, sorry Cuz, it isn't terminal, just had to get in touch with my higher sensibilities for a bit. Promise I won't do it again … after I say this. Thanks for always guarding my back.

My editor gave me specific orders not to thank every outfitter who has been a part of this book, but just because they aren't named here doesn't mean that they don't belong. Thanks all of you, and one special thanks to Fred Webb, arctic legend and friend.

To all of you wilderness guides who have shared your tents, "wickies," lean-tos, tarps and igloos with me, thanks. Without your knowledge of the wild lands, my stories would have

many more unhappy endings.

To every horse that I've ridden, ha-ha, in spite of your best efforts, I'm still alive!

My editor also says that I don't have space to thank every writer/editor who has helped me with my writing (John Zent), inspiration (Judd Cooney), guidance (Jim Zumbo), sage council (Craig Boddington), opportunity … too many to thank and to many, thanks.

Without the support of the "industry" — the manufacturers who keep us in hunting goods — this book couldn't have happened. Bill Jordan, Bob Nosler and Leupold's Mike Slack, thank you for believing in me. And although there are too many others to acknowledge here, I have to especially thank all of the good people at Knight Muzzleloading, past and present, including the Watley's and Brian Harrington and, finally, the man himself, Tony Knight, my good friend, mentor and the genius behind the muzzleloading revolution.

The writing in this book can be divided into my pre-Gregg Gutschow writing and my post-Gregg Gutschow writing. The latter is infinitely better. For the last 10 years, Attila the Editor has hacked and slashed my best prose into the comely shape you hold in your hands. It pains me to admit it, but he was right every single dangling passive participle time! Thanks, Gregg; thanks for editing my best and worst and, more importantly, thanks for the friendship.

Now for the hardest part, for how do you give thanks for life? There is no adequate way, at least not with words. But beyond the wild lands somewhere, there is a place where I will end up and where I will be able to pay my deepest respects. There already await many from the pages of this book. In time, we will all be together again and will forever relive past hunts. ■

CONTENTS

Introduction 5

Foreword 6

PART I: HUNTING ON THE RAGGED EDGE

Chapter One: Imagine A Land 8

Chapter Two: The Edge Of Insanity 18

Chapter Three: Facing Down Fear 24

Chapter Four: Diary Of Despair 32

Chapter Five: Epilogue: Danger Knocks 42

PART II: MAN AGAINST BEAST

Chapter Six: Come Hell Or High Water 50

Chapter Seven: On The Trail Of Danger 58

Chapter Eight: Ol' Three Legs 64

Chapter Nine: The Hunted 68

Chapter Ten: The Ring Of Fire 76

PART III: OH DEER!

Chapter Eleven: Toe-To-Toe 84

Chapter Twelve: The Fire In His Eye 88

Chapter Thirteen: 'Big' Kodiak Deer Hunt 92

Chapter Fourteen: The Baddest Blacktail 96

PART IV: ANTLER KINGS

Chapter Fifteen: White Manes & Blackpowder 104

Chapter Sixteen: Nord By Northeast 110

Chapter Seventeen: Diary Of A Yukon Odyssey 116

Chapter Eighteen: He Could Charge At Any Second! 122

Chapter Nineteen: Behind The Scenes For Shiras Moose ...128

Chapter Twenty: Valley Of The Moose 134

PART V: MOUNTAIN MYSTERIES

Chapter Twenty-One: Bulls And Billies 140

Chapter Twenty-Two: Hunting The Devil's Bath 146

Chapter Twenty-Three: Climbing Solo 152

Chapter Twenty-Four: Up & Down Mountain Goats 156

INTRODUCTION

Why? Why travel hundreds of thousands of miles, by airplane, truck, boat, dogsled, horse and foot and spend the better part of two decades (a goodly part of this lifetime) in some out-of-the-way, often God-forsaken "where," searching for … "what?" Good question, one best answered with "who" … who I was, who I am and who I desire to be.

Personally I didn't think that I was weird when I was growing up; a little obsessive and childishly self-centered perhaps, but not weird. At least not weird if collecting bugs, chasing gophers, raising snakes and catching mice, frogs and salamanders is normal. The greatest day of my young life (except for high school graduation) had nothing to do with a first kiss or my first straight "B" report card or winning a swimming race; nope, it was the day that I out-witted and tagged my first white-tailed buck. Is that weird? Maybe, but that's who I was.

If there was a weird part of my life, it would have to be the years during which I attended university (Canadian for college). During those years, the truth be known, I dabbled with being "more normal," experimented with socially acceptable behavior as it were. It didn't work. While the "in" gang played the game, I dreamed of wild game. The happiest day of my young adult life, (except for college graduation), was the day that my deer rifle was delivered to my dormitory, carefully packed and shipped by my father. Thanks, Dad, for the life ring.

Some might even consider the "who" I am today a little strange, but really I am the same person I was yesterday. I'm still a little obsessive and self-centered, but now with two wonderful teenage children, two dogs, two cats, a home, a pre-94 Mighty Dodge and a true love, my wife, whom I worship and whose friendship I cherish. If that's considered strange these days, so be it. Instead of chasing frogs and snakes, I travel the continent, indeed the world, searching for … adventure … sort of; in reality searching for something deeper, something that in a conundrum-kind-of-way, can only be found inside … but that only exists outside. Ask any hunter, he'll know what it means.

Oddly it wasn't a particular animal that I

hunted hardest for, it was the inside things that took the longest to find. Things like searching inside myself for the patience of my Inuit friends. Not the patience of waiting in a line for your turn, but the patience of the People, the patience of living "on the land." That took five journeys to the arctic, a dozen blizzards, two broken sleds, no food and bad ice before I finally "got it." Took about the same amount of time and a broken satellite phone to communicate properly with my loved ones. I was on a sheep mountain, poised on the height of land, pining. My Dene Cree guide sat beside me and told me to look at the moon, said it was the same moon that we all share. It was probably the first time that I ever really understood what it means to be spiritual.

So to answer the original question, "Why travel hundreds of thousands of miles, by airplane, truck, boat, dogsled, horse and foot and spend the better part of two decades in some out-of-the-way, often God-forsaken 'where' searching for … 'what?'" Simple, because I was born a hunter, I am a hunter and I always will be a hunter. ■

■ FOREWORD

adventure—an undertaking involving danger and unknown risks.

You need not search for danger in this book. It will find you. Unknown risk, you ask? Consider that no one until Jim Shockey had ever set foot to tundra or mountain granite with a blackpowder firearm in hand questing each of the continent's big game species.

Author Shockey epitomizes and captures ultimate North American hunting adventure to its razor's edge. From an igloo tomb in the arctic, to a mountain goat glacier in British Columbia, to a brown bear alder jungle on a volcanic island. He scintillates and titillates. He frightens and laughs. He reflects, respects and reveres. And he absolutely never quits. Never. Grit, determination, passion … call it what you will. He is driven by something that flows in his blood, that something that only we hunters sense, that same something we struggle to define.

Moreover, God gifted this man with a flair to chart his course with inspired, sometimes spiritual prose that goes to the heart of the hunt and whisks us to the edge of oblivion.

Innumerable are the times that I've sat in my warm, comfortable magazine editor's chair and received a raw Jim Shockey feature article manuscript to consider for an upcoming issue and torn at the envelope with abandon to escape along with him. And even before I knew it, I stared chillingly at 13 steps into the beady black eyes of a man-killer grizzly. Before I could stop, I'd be fighting for my life in a midnight arctic blizzard dozens of miles from safety and thousands of miles from my family. Before I could free myself from his grip, I'd teeter on the precipice of a jagged mountain cliff staring at a majestic wild ram with all of my camp and provisions on my back. I could smell it, breathe it, taste it, suffer it in Jim's words. It was all there every time. I longed for nothing.

My admiration for Jim's writing eventually turned into a friendship because it became clear to me immediately that Jim "got it." Beneath the firestorm of adventure that racks his writing are the underpinnings of hunting tradition and

culture. This is not some guy hell-bent for heads. Certainly, he has spent dearly. So has he sacrificed. He'd tell you, though, that the substantial cost has been, by compare, inconsequential to the dividends. It is clear that this is a guy grateful to have been born a hunter—someone comfortable in a mountain tent alone or an igloo with Inuit friends reveling in ancient Inuit legend. He is someone who, like many of us, has taken turns in his life and set his sights on

something else. He's been enormously success-ful, but has at the same time always utterly failed to abandon the hunt for long.

Today the best of the best of Jim's hunting journeys reside here fully illustrated with the images that he burned to film from all of those wild, inhospitable places. It is possible, I sup-pose, that you might still somehow be unfamil-iar with this man and his writing. If that is the case, you are in for an odyssey and by the end, I believe, will consider yourself fortunate to have re-traced his footsteps across North America. If, like me, you've come to know Jim Shockey through his writings published in the foremost hunting magazines, you can collect here the pieces of the complex puzzle that you might have been missing.

For if you've lamented the lack of a book that completely defines hunting adventure, Jim Shockey has now written it. ∎

CHAPTER ONE:
IMAGINE A

LAND

Imagine a land without fences, without bounds; a land where forever is as close as the horizon, a land where the sun never sets. Imagine a land that explodes into life and color for one month of the year, where all plant life is compressed by necessity into that one month. Germinate, bud, leaf, flower and seed, the entire alternation of generations within the same time span that a normal plant gently warms under April showers.

Such a land exists; it is the living arctic of the summer.

Now imagine the same land, frozen, cold, locked in ice; imagine the dead arctic of the winter, a land where the sun never rises. The arctic during this time becomes a land bounded at every choice by that very thin line that separates life from death. Forever is not so far away as the horizon, it's as close as the next misstep.

Still.

Silent.

It's a land resolute during those times when the tendrils of snow shift and curl soundlessly across the ice, foreshadowing the inevitable; the blizzard is coming. The arctic during the winter is a land at once benign and sinister. A psychotic

The rules are different in the arctic. Sometimes beautiful and serene, other times a killer, the arctic does not forgive small mistakes. To adventurers, it is spell-binding.

land that whispers one second and SCREAMS the next. It becomes a land tortured to the depths of its perma-frosted soul when the blizzard rages. Enduring is the only option when the snow blasts insanely across the icy reaches. Hunker down and endure. Home is where you are.

REAL DANGER

Make no mistake. The danger is real. I know this first hand. I've hunted the arctic many times and suffered in the clutches of the "blizzard violent." Once during a muskox hunt, one detailed later in this chapter, my hunting party attempted to get back to the nearest Inuit village of Kugluktuk for five days, to no avail. We needed to go tens of miles, but succeeded in traveling less than a dozen. Finally, out of fuel and beaten, we were forced into our tents. Rescue became the only option.

The wind in the arctic is a wild thing; it breaches every crack, fills every fissure with biting cold. Your breath shakes and quakes as it wafts from your cold lips, inside the tent. It was the wind that was the worst on that trip. It roared and whistled, moaned and cried and

then lowed, gently, giving hope to the hopeless. But it was a lie. Just when it seemed the worst was over, it would scream once again. Never trust the arctic wind.

Thankfully, the hunt had a happy ending, and the rescue party eventually reached us. But the memory darkens this day with melancholy. As I write this, I'm preparing for a polar bear hunt—a hunt that might keep me up to a month out on the pack ice of the Arctic Ocean. My Inuit guide and I will be traveling by dog team for hundreds of miles across the flow, to where we hope to find the open water leads used by seals and, by course, polar bears.

As I write of it, days before I embark on the adventure, my Inuit guide and his helper are out on the ice setting up a temporary base camp of ice blocks and canvas tents. A simple process in a more hospitable clime, but in the arctic, where forever is as close as the next misstep, sadly, such is not the case. Nothing is simple here.

One year ago, almost to the day, two Inuit from another community went out onto the ice on their snow machines, ostensibly to do exactly what my guides are doing for me. The first

night, 75 miles from the village, they stopped and set up camp. It happened as they brewed their coffee inside the canvas tent … the white gas camper stove flared. In the time it takes to tell it, the tent was on fire!

The two Inuit guides, clad only in their sweaters and light jackets, escaped what instantly became an inferno when the small camp-stove exploded. They didn't have time to pull their traveling clothing, sleeping gear or even one of the caribou sleeping mats from the flames. Everything was consumed, save the two snow machines.

I remember well the phone call from Fred Webb, the legendary arctic outfitter and friend with whom I've hunted many times.

"Jim, I'm not sure we're going to be running your polar bear hunt next year," he paused, a hard man choked up. "One of my guides didn't make it back to town yesterday."

The arctic is a harsh taskmaster. Properly equipped, even in terrible temperatures, travel is possible. Ill-equipped as the two unfortunate guides were, travel is absolutely a last resort. For them, it was the last resort. One, the older Inuit, made it back to the village, but the other died after what could only have been an indescribably cold race for survival. The search party found the brave man's body 15 miles from the village.

THE ALLURE

If the arctic is a harsh taskmaster, it is also, in the bizarre dichotomy of character that defines the arctic, a siren of sorts. It isn't so much "song" that it uses to catch the adventurer, as it is "touch;" once touched by the frigid breath of this barely imaginable land, the hunter will return. The hunter has to return, and so will I. Fred is running his polar bear hunts this year and will, as surely as the arctic wind portends ill, be running them again next year.

Truly, hunting the arctic is an experience that every hunter with an adventurous spirit should try at least once. Arguably, it's the last frontier left on the North American continent, the last for the hunter to explore. Yes, the arctic must be

Arctic animals are fearless. Man seems inconsequential compared to the environment.

Chapter One: Imagine a Land

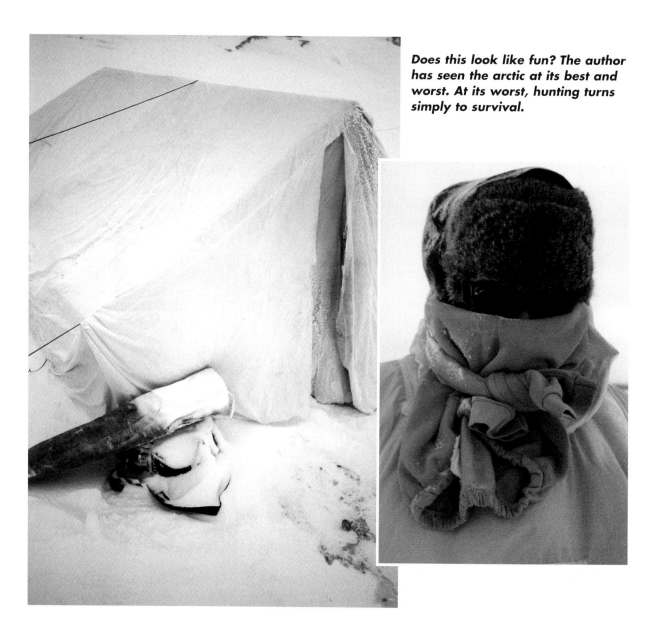

taken seriously and every step calculated, but hunts rarely end tragically, especially with outfitters like Fred Webb.

Fred takes every precaution to ensure the safety of his hunters. Every Inuit guide is equipped with a single side-band radio and Global Positioning System (GPS) unit. Plus, Fred maintains a residence in the arctic from where he can monitor all of the hunting teams on the tundra or ice. Today, satellite telephones, only slightly larger than the typical cell phone, take arctic communication to Space Age levels. While still an adventure fraught with the unexpected, as it must be by definition, help is now a phone call away.

Knowing all this, the arctic hunter can crawl into the sled box, and from the very first minute, enjoy the experience. There's nothing down South to compare with bumping across the rock-hard snow, frozen in tiny waves as far as the eye can see. Nothing to compare with your first "whiteout;" the arctic version of oblivion. The world might be standing on end, and then again it might not. Things far away will appear close and things close, far; nothing makes sense, literally, when your senses fail you. Actually, "nothingness" is a good way to describe the arctic landscape during a severe whiteout.

"Haunting" would be another word to describe a whiteout, except that it's a word that better describes the "northern lights" that every

ANIMALS OF THE ARCTIC

MUSKOX:

Presently muskox numbers are high enough to allow for both a sport hunt and a commercial hunt. The hunter can expect to see tens and possibly hundreds of these unusual creatures. A muskox hunt is a perfect choice for the hunter venturing into the arctic for the first time. Hunts generally take place in March, April or late fall.

ARCTIC ISLAND CARIBOU:

These beautiful and petite white caribou are normally hunted on Victoria Island and can often be hunted in the fall in conjunction with muskox.

BARREN GROUND GRIZZLY:

Surprisingly, the barren grounds are the home to a high population of barren ground grizzly bears. Beginning in April, these ferocious animals leave their dens and travel across the snow-covered tundra, in search of food. Hunts take place in April and May.

POLAR BEAR:

Contrary to what many believe, polar bears are not endangered. There is a healthy population in the arctic, and Inuit hunters are allowed to guide for and hunt for these largest of the world's carnivores. As this is written, polar bears may be imported into the United States if they are taken from specified areas. Hunts take place during March, April and May and non-Inuit hunters must use dog team and sled, not snow machines.

ATLANTIC WALRUS:

Until very recently, walrus hunting of any species was prohibited. But as this is written, biologists have determined that the population of Atlantic walrus is high enough to allow a sport hunt. Currently, the walrus can not be imported into the United States, but there is hope that this will change in time. This under-rated and overlooked hunt is truly adventure hunting at its best. Walrus are hunted on the icepack during July and August.

arctic hunter is sure to see. On clear nights, the hunter will stand breathless beneath a night sky alive with ethereal dancers. They'll wave and shift, glow and fade and then burst forth in color. Haunting. Magnificent. God? Experiencing the northern lights will leave the most traveled hunter humbled.

And once that hunter has taken in as much otherworldly pageantry as his "put in place" mortal soul can handle, the tent awaits. There he'll enjoy a fine meal of boiled something or other (sometimes it's better not to ask), and take part in a nightly arctic ritual—listening to the heartbeat of the arctic, the single side-band radio. From here and there across the arctic, those Inuit "on the land" will touch base with friends and family waiting for word back in the village. Some of the distorted conversations, those in English, the hunter will be able to follow, and some he will not, but, as if the hunter has become part of a greater arctic social unconscious, all will make sense.

Or it will until suddenly, on cue, all human conversation will cease and an eerie sound will pervade the airwaves. "What is that?" the hunter will ask, and the Inuit will quietly and with reverence, explain that the "old people" are talking. They won't want to continue the conversation, but if pushed, they'll say that the "old people" are the ancestors, the people who've come and gone before. Whether it's to save batteries or as a show of respect I'm not sure, but the guide will reach over and turn the radio off

14

For all of its hardship, for all of the inherent risks, an arctic adventure's rewards might be the sweetest that the North American continent can offer. Comparatively few hunters venture here, but those who do find a land and a people who will haunt their memories forever.

first and the lantern next. It is time to sleep.

Oddly, no matter how cold it is outside, inside the tent, heated only by a tiny stove and lantern, it will feel warm. Buried deep inside a sleeping bag of wondrous proportions, the hunter will be positively roasting. Beneath the bag, the dried (but not tanned) hides of several beasts, caribou and muskox, will protect guide and hunter from the ice and snow floor. Sleep comes easily in the arctic; the morrow waits, and with it, adventure! These are the things that define the arctic's allure.

SURVIVAL

All things being equal, the chances of survival are directly proportional to the desire to survive. In other words, equally outfitted with gear, be it adequate or less than adequate, if two humans of equal conditioning are faced with a survival situation, the one who has the strongest will to survive will have the greatest chance of doing so.

That said, the biggest problem I've seen among non-Inuit, myself included, is our orientation to the calendar and the clock. We self-impose deadlines that dictate where and when we have to be somewhere. I daresay that more hunters have been killed by "get-home-itis" than by anything else. In the arctic, home is where you are when the bad weather hits. That

"grand opening" you were scheduled to attend isn't worth your life. Sit tight and wait, days if necessary. The weather will get better.

Cold weather gear, of course, is essential for a hunter's survival. The Inuit will provide the hunter with native clothing of caribou skins and fur, but trust me; they are a far hardier people than we are. The fur-clothing looks exotic in photos and will do in a pinch, but a non-Inuit hunter would do himself a big favor in the survival department if he purchased a set of arctic expedition gear like that made by Northern Outfitters.

HUNTING THE ARCTIC

Typically, an arctic hunt will entail travel and glassing. The North is vast—thousands of miles wide by the same deep—and the animals can be few and far between, depending on what the hunter is looking for. From this or that vantage, the Inuit will stop and glass through the arctic's version of heat waves. Herds of muskox and caribou will hove to in sharp contrast with the white land. Wolverines, great white tundra wolves and occasionally polar bears will stand defiant in the glass lenses.

It truly is an amazing thing to see these animals; some like the muskox, leftovers from the last ice age, stand as a living description of the

arctic. Their great shaggy, brown-silver coats brush the ground and their massive, corrugated bosses and ivory horn tips speak of things ancient and eternal. They aren't going any-where, a bold statement justified by way of hard-won survival.

Others like the great white tundra wolves, speak more of remarkable adaptation to the harsh climate. They're bigger than their Southern cousins and, I daresay, twice as tough when their ire is raised. They have to be, or how else could they hope to bring down a calf muskox from the center of a circled herd of ani-mals that have evolved to survive far more fero-cious onslaughts from the likes of prehistoric animals like cave bears and saber-toothed tigers!

Furtive isn't in the vocabulary of the denizens of the North. Why hide? It's not like there's a forest nearby or a swamp to disappear into. The creatures that the hunter will be hunting don't hide, and for this they cannot be faulted. Nor should they be judged by the same standards that Southern game animals are judged. They live in a different type of habitat with a different set of rules for survival. The "hunting" isn't so much a cat and mouse game of whitetailesque "peek-a-boo," it's more an exercise of the hunter's desire.

Arctic hunts do not happen because the hunter has a weekend free. They happen because the hunter takes the time and makes the effort to make it happen. Such a hunt takes months and sometimes, as in the case of a polar bear hunt, years of preparation and planning. In the paradoxical way that the arctic exists, the hunter has to desire adventure or he'll never see the animal that doesn't hide.

So is it worth it? Is it worth foregoing comfort? Is it worth risking … well, everything? Ask any hunter who's been to the arctic. He'll go quiet for a moment, reflecting upon the still and the cold, the northern lights and the land that's nearly unimaginable for those who've never been, and then he'll answer your question. He'll answer it the only way any hunter who's been touched by the breath of the arctic can. ■

CHAPTER TWO:

THE EDGE OF INSANITY

Night had become day, day had become night. Time had become a relative thing, measured only by the ebb and flow of the bitter north wind. It would howl and roar with a vengeance and then abate and grow quiet. My Inuit guide, John Franklin Kaoloak, would cock his head and listen. Was the blizzard finally over?

During those times when the wind stopped trying to rip us from the tent, it would instead whisper sinister across the land like a lie, "Come out and play little ones, I've changed. See how gentle I can be? I won't hurt you ... you paltry, insignificant nothings! HOW DARE YOU ENTER MY DOMAIN!

WHAM!

Suddenly, wild and screaming like a banshee, the wind would hammer into our tent camp, forcing itself upon our small party of six adventurers. And so another time would pass, the three small, canvas tents shuddering and heaving against their anchoring and every loose bit of tarp battering itself to shreds in the wind.

Oddly, in spite of the blizzard's force, I was happy; I'd come north seeking a hunting adventure and by every conceivable measure, I'd found one. The Boone and Crockett Club (B&C) record-book muskox that I'd killed with my Knight muzzleloader on the second day of the hunt—the last nice day—was the cake, and the knowledge that we'd tried and almost reached the legendary Bluenose caribou herd was the icing.

I'd first learned of the Bluenose herd in college and then again from outfitter Fred Webb while hunting at his Courageous Lake caribou camp in the Northwest Territories in 1994. That hunt had been comfortable, safe and incredible. While I was there, caribou by the thousands trailed past the camp, just like they

In an all-out arctic blizzard, man's technology helps, but man's judgment ultimately determines his fate.

poses, been sport hunted. Fred told of seeing Bluenose caribou racks—racks that easily surpassed the existing B&C world record—lying around Coppermine, Northwest Territories. When I expressed interest, he mentioned that, starting in 1995, he was going to offer a combination Bluenose caribou and muskox late-fall hunt. He told me that getting a muskox should be easy, but added that I shouldn't get too excited because trying to reach the Bluenose herd might end up being more of an adventure than a hunt. Little did we know how prophetic Fred's words were to become.

THE SEARCH FOR HOPE LAKE

Now, a year later, I was five days into that hunt, and it had become an adventure. After I killed my muskox, the weather took a turn for the worse; it started snowing ... and snowing … and snowing. Three times in the three days since I'd killed my muskox we'd broken camp, loaded the sleds and headed into the white nothingness, trying to make it to a place aptly named Hope Lake. The guides knew of a trapper cabin there, a place where we could sit out the bad weather in relative safety.

During those three aborted attempts to reach Hope Lake, we traveled in absolute whiteout

do every year. But then I hadn't expected anything different. From the extensive research that I'd done on Fred's Courageous Lake operation, I knew that the record book is written testimony to Fred's success at guiding for giant caribou.

During my 1994 hunt with Fred, I'd already killed two record-book bulls with my Knight muzzleloader and was so impressed with the professional way that he ran his outfit, that I'd decided to book a muskox hunt with him. It was while I was quizzing him about the muskox hunts he offered, that he inadvertently mentioned the Bluenose caribou herd.

This little-known herd resides in Fred's hunting area and had never, for all intents and pur-

Via a fuzzy radio connection, the author's hunting team received reports about attempts to rescue them. When the rescuers arrived, 47 tortuous miles remained to safety.

conditions and, in a way, it was like flying through a cloud. There was no forward, no backward and no up or down. The snow machine in front would seem to rise eerily in mid-air and then float down. But there was no way of knowing whether that machine was climbing a hill or if your machine was going down one.

My snow machine had broken down on the third day, so we left it cached with the muskox meat and from then on, I rode on the sled John, one of my Inuit guides, was pulling. Since it was too cold to look forward into the wind, I stared off to the side, into the endless white, trying to see some landmark, some distant height of land … anything. Suddenly, my eyes would focus on something closer, much closer, something huge passing right in front of my face! To my shock, I would realize that I'd been staring the whole time into a snow bank a dozen feet away.

John and the two other Inuit guides, Peter Katiak and George Haniliak, kept us from pitching head first off one of those sky-high snow banks, but they couldn't avoid the deep powder snow that bogged the heavily loaded sleds down every few hundred yards. When a sled got stuck, we'd all pitch in and push. Many times, even with three machines pulling and the three of us hunters pushing (myself, Lynn Herbert of

Oregon and Jimmie Rosenbruch of Alaska), the mired sled would just barely heave free. As the snow deepened, we began jettisoning nonessentials to lighten the sleds. The guides would take a GPS reading at each cache so they could retrieve the gear sometime in the future.

Finally, in spite of a super-human effort by the Inuit guides, on our third day of trying to reach the cabin at Hope Lake, we were forced to give up. What should have taken three hours in good weather, had taken us three days, and we were still 10 impossible miles short of our destination. Even if we'd have wanted to, we couldn't have continued on; the bad weather had turned into a full-blown blizzard. And in trying to reach Hope Lake, we'd used almost all the remaining gasoline. We only had enough gas left to fill the tank of one snow machine.

Still, even though things weren't going as planned, we weren't in the dire straights that we could have been. On the positive side, we knew exactly where we were; I had my own GPS unit, and our Inuit guides had two more. We knew that we were exactly 47 air miles from the safety of Coppermine, the village we'd departed five days before.

We were also able to make fuzzy radio contact with Fred in Coppermine. So, more importantly

than us knowing where we were, someone from the outside world knew where we were, too. Over the single side-band radio, Fred informed us that he'd send a rescue team out from Coppermine, into the blizzard, with more gasoline. He informed us to stand by for progress reports.

HUNT TURNS TO RESCUE

It was a full day later when Fred came back on the air. Things were starting to get exciting. Our rescue party had returned to Coppermine saying that the snow was too deep. Fred informed us that our two Inuit rescuers were re-outfitting themselves, both with more powerful long-track snow machines, and also with smaller, lighter sleds. Fred's crackling voice told us that the party would be on its way again shortly and that we should stand by once more.

We were, by then, into the sixth day of our adventure and we all knew that our options were limited. Not that we couldn't have lasted several more days. Food-wise, we could have. The guides had killed a caribou cow, and we were enjoying some of the finest raw caribou steaks to be had anywhere south of the North Pole.

It was noon on the seventh day of the adventure when Fred's voice once again broke through the radio static. The blizzard had abated slightly, but in spite of the good weather news, the news from Fred was bad. The rescue party was bogged down 40 miles short of our position. They were unable to continue and needed one of us to break a trail to them.

It was John, my Inuit guide, who took down the rescue party's GPS coordinates and went out into the cold to pour the last of our gasoline into his machine's gas tank. On the bright side, he wouldn't be pulling a heavy sled through the deep snow, so we knew that he should be able to make substantially better time than we'd been able to. But on the dark side, if John's machine broke down or if he ran off a cliff, he'd be caught in the blistering cold without any survival gear. When John disappeared into the never-ending white nothingness, I can't honestly say I was panicking quite yet, but I was concerned for the safety of my brave, young Inuit guide.

The author's muskox hunt began well enough, with relatively warm sunshine and a huge bull. Then he witnessed how the arctic can turn on you.

The hours dragged by that day like they were weighted with lead. By 7 p.m., when Peter and George shot the first flare into the sky, it had already been pitch black for three hours. At 8, they shot off another flare and then another at 9. It wasn't until 10 p.m., 10 hours after John left us, that we finally saw the welcome flash of his headlight. Unbelievably, he had traveled more than 80 miles, half of the time in whiteout conditions and the other half in darkness. He'd done it! We were saved!

More or less.

John might have done the near impossible, finding and then bringing the rescue party back to us, but the weather was worsening again. John, soaking wet and exhausted from the journey, also informed us that the snow was deeper farther on. If we expected to get out before spring, it had to be that night. So we broke camp in darkness, loaded up the sleds and headed into the black arctic midnight.

Memories of that long, cold night and the next day, come back to me now dim and disjointed. We traveled without resting. I remember push-

ing and pulling heavy bogged sleds until my muscles ached. I remember trying to walk in waist-deep snow and being so tired that I finally just flopped back in the snow and closed my eyes for a few minutes. I remember being utterly alone in the blackest night that I have ever seen. The snow machines and my hunting partners had gone on ahead; the machines had to be hitched in tandem and were hauling the other two sleds ahead several miles. I knew that they would eventually come back for my sled and me. Eventually.

During that long, black night, we had to jettison almost all the rest of our gear. We even left one of the sleds behind. In the end, 24 hours after John left to find the rescue party, we finally cleared the last rise and saw the village of Coppermine. By then, we only had one small tent and one sleeping bag left between all of us. If we wouldn't have made it ... but we did. ■

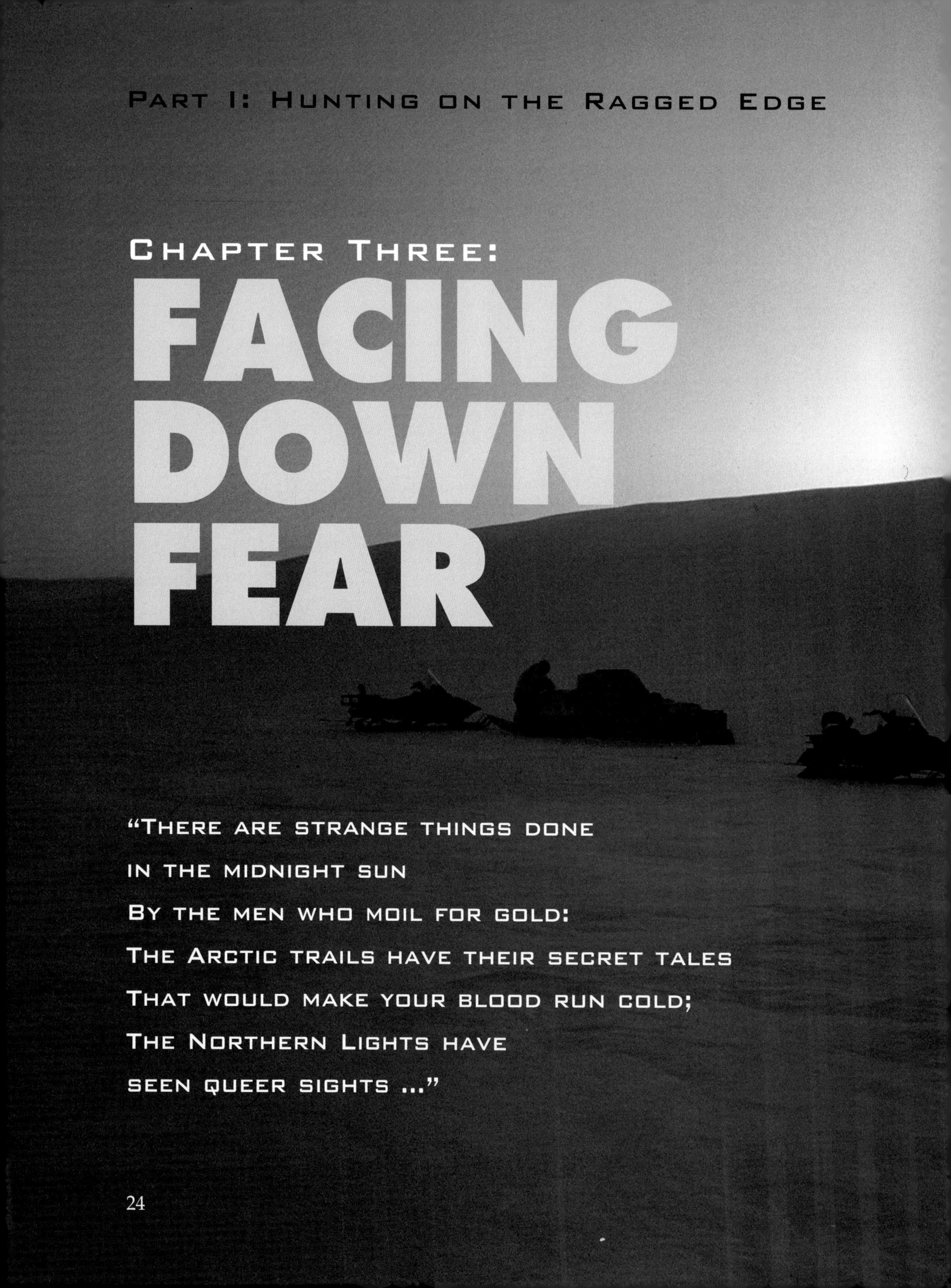

CHAPTER THREE:
FACING DOWN FEAR

"THERE ARE STRANGE THINGS DONE

IN THE MIDNIGHT SUN

BY THE MEN WHO MOIL FOR GOLD:

THE ARCTIC TRAILS HAVE THEIR SECRET TALES

THAT WOULD MAKE YOUR BLOOD RUN COLD;

THE NORTHERN LIGHTS HAVE

SEEN QUEER SIGHTS ..."

When you stand quiet and alone in the bitter-cold, black arctic night, the words of poet Robert Service can never be far from your mind. He was there. Maybe it was 100 years ago, but he was there. Besides, in the arctic, that was yesterday; his dogsled tracks no doubt still lie, like a blue line upon the vast, wild land, proof of his passage. Nothing changes in the arctic. Time is frozen.

"Talk of your cold through the parka's fold it stabbed like a driven nail. If our eyes we'd close, then the lashes froze till sometimes we couldn't see ..."

I can tell you why I was in the arctic—to hunt muskox—but don't ask me why I was standing there under the stars, high on the snow-covered hill that protected our insignificant tent camp from a blizzardy flanking attack. Maybe like getting on a horse that had just thrown me, I was facing a fear. Eighteen months earlier near this very place, I'd wondered whether my first

muskox hunt in the arctic might be my last. Those memories and bits and pieces of Service crossed my mind as I stood there watching Hale-Bopp cross the arctic night sky.

But the arctic deceives. Yes, the night sky was crystal clear, benign and in a frigid, "I love you but not tonight" kind of way; but I knew better. Crystal-clear all right, like black ice. I knew only too well how treacherous the outlands can be, how instantly this place can turn on you.

"It's the cursed cold, and it's got right hold
till I'm chilled clean through to the bone
Yet 'taint being dead — it's my awful dread
of the icy grave that pains ..."

I knew of the violence lurking just beyond sight, over the horizon. During my last trip here, I suffered the wrath and fury of an arctic gone berserk. I killed a muskox with my Knight muzzleloader on day two of that hunt, but even as my Inuit guide and I finished quartering the primitive beast, the weather deteriorated.

"And on I went, though the dogs were spent
and the grub was getting low.

Shaken after his first muskox adventure, the author returned to the arctic for muskox. This time he saw her in all her splendor.

The trail was bad, and I felt half mad,
but I swore I would not give in ..."

That first hunt had been an experimental fall hunt set up as a combination hunt for caribou. But now, standing there on that hill in March, it didn't seem like this could be the same arctic. Fred Webb told me when I booked this second muskox hunt with him that, with any luck, the weather should be better than my previous hunt. Better? I guess it was better! When I stepped off of the NWT Air turbo prop in Kugluktuk, I expected hula girls to be giving out flower leighs!

The temperature was a balmy minus 20, and the wind that had been vicious and blinding 18 months before, was "fresh" but not insufferable. In other words, if a fellow had been foolish enough to expose his nose, it would have taken at least 15 minutes for the protruding proboscis to freeze off.

I had no intention of exposing my proboscis or any other part of my body to the elements during this hunt. On the first hunt I'd worn all the give-away cold weather gear that I could borrow from my relatives back on the prairies. But for this hunt I was dressed in the latest high-tech arctic expedition clothing made by Northern Outfitters. Based on my prior experience, I wasn't about to get caught with my hydrophobic, insulation matrix Vatrex long johns down. This time, too, I brought along a case of HotHands disposable handwarmers.

"Maybe we'll have some good weather this time," Fred said, eyes twinkling as he held out his hand in greeting. "Get your bags, you'll be heading out this afternoon."

Within the hour I had my hunting license and tag, and Fred was introducing me to the Inuit guides for the adventure: Charlie Bolt, Jack Atatahak and his grandson, B.J. He also introduced me to the other two hunters: Mike VanHandel from Wisconsin and Eric Llanes from New York.

A Turn for the Better

The sun was still shining as our guides climbed their snow machines and we climbed aboard the sleds they pulled. It was so gloriously sunny that I actually had to wear sunglasses!

For several hours and 50 miles, we raced over the tundra, bumped across frozen bays and passed by other waving Inuit hunters and fishermen. Then it was up into the higher icy reaches where the largest of the muskox reside. Huge jagged rocks, left over from the last Ice Age like so many billion tons of prehistoric litter, began to protrude from the snow here and there and, eventually, everywhere; forcing our guides to slow down and pick their way.

When we stopped for tea, I was informed that the oldest bulls preferred this God-forgotten rocky terrain because when wolves attacked, the muskox would back up against the jagged rocks and leave the cunning canines only one option, a full frontal attack. Not a wise choice

for a wolf unless that wolf was sitting at the controls of a D-10 Caterpillar.

Onward that day we forged, miles more, though indeed more carefully and not by a sight near full speed ahead. And it was in the dark of that first night, after stopping to set up our canvas tents in the snow and dining on delicious boiled caribou, that I slipped out to reflect under the alien promise of Hale-Bopp's glare.

"I do not know how long in the snow
I wrestled with grisly fear:
But the stars came out and they danced about
ere again I ventured near ..."

Two of the three tents, lighted like dim giant night lights, had already blinked out by the time I kneeled and crawled through the door of my own still-bright tent. My Inuit guide was just turning off the single side-band radio for the night. I doffed my gear and climbed onto the foot-deep matting of stiff, dried caribou and muskox hides covering the snow. It wasn't until then, as the lantern hissed itself out, that I

began to feel hope. Lying there in half sleep I could still hear Service out there somewhere.

"And that very night, as we lay packed tight
in our robes beneath the snow,
And the dogs were fed, and the stars o'erhead
were dancing heel and toe ..."

I was startled awake by the silence. It was morning, that was obvious, but where was the wind that I'd grown used to on my first hunt? Though I'd sworn I wouldn't do it, I crawled out of my sleeping bag and stuck my proboscis outside. There was no wind! None! And not a cloud in the sky.

MUSKOX GALORE

Never was there a more glorious day to hunt muskox in the arctic. We put miles on, spied 100 muskox, maybe more, I lost count. Through our binoculars, across miles and through the arctic's version of heatwaves, several of the largest muskox looked big enough to go after.

The next morning, and, in fact, every morning for the duration of the hunt, dawned bright and

All of the hunters in the author's party took giant, record-book muskox bulls during the hunt with outfitter Fred Webb. Judging for trophy size was the largest challenge.

sunny. The rising sun promised a good day, a big day and like a debt paid, it was. As soon as we finished breakfast the second day, we loaded up and headed after one of the groups of bulls that we'd seen the day before, but we didn't get there.

Before we'd rounded the first line of rocky ridges, the lead sled slid to a stop. It was obvious that our guides had seen something miles away across the valley, and so, while they planned, we three "umingnok" hunters pow-wowed. Since I'd already been, I offered to let the other two hunters shoot first. Eric won the toss and with the rest of us in tow, commenced, with his guide, to stalk a bachelor group of three old bulls. All would have qualified for the B&C record book, but one was a giant among muskox.

When the rifle cracked in the dense arctic air, there was one muskox down and two to go.

We didn't hunt the rest of that day. Our guides decided that we could find older bulls than the two remaining with their fallen comrade. This suited Mike and I, but didn't seem to please the two decidedly aggressive muskox bulls; it took some effort to persuade them to vacate the area. By the time they left and we retrieved the snow machines and butchered the bull, it was time to return to camp.

A WORLD RECORD FALLS

The next day was another arctic dream. The sun shone and shone. We could see for dozens of miles in every direction and we could see dozens upon dozens of muskox. Two here, five there and 100 just beyond. Every time we spotted a herd of the beasts, it was impossible to ignore the feeling that we'd just been transported back in time to the last Ice Age. It was obvious that none of the great, shaggy creatures had ever seen a busload of tourists.

Grand day that it was, it wasn't until the next day that we actually spotted what we were looking for: a herd of 12 bulls traveling together. Even from a great distance, with my untrained eye and the help of my excellent Leupold optics, I could see that every one of the bulls would make the B&C book!

We planned and made our stalk without further adieu. Mike was the shooter and was faced with the "cry me a river" problem of picking the bull he felt was the largest of the bunch. To which I wished him good luck. Every bull in the bunch was a monster.

A man of action, Mike wasted not a moment once we managed to sneak to within shooting range.

Ka-BOOM! Two down, one to go.

I, unlike Mike, when suddenly faced with 11 choices became a man incapable of decision. Hemmm. Hawwww. Hemmm. Hawwww. My guide just shook his head as the whole herd eventually decided to bolt.

Fortunately, the bulls chose the long "slow-cut" over the ridge, while my guide and I ran

At the time, the author's bull earned a place in the Longhunter Society records as the largest muskox ever taken by a hunter using a muzzle-loader.

for the shortcut. We beat the bulls. Barely. And again I almost hemmed and hawed the opportunity away. It took a direct order from my guide, just as the last bull turned to wheel, to make me squeeze the trigger.

The bull looked huge in the scope, but when I walked up to him, he wasn't. If there is such a word, he was huger! So huge in fact that even without measuring I could tell he was easily the new muzzleloading world record.

As my guide crunched across the tundra to fetch the snow machine, I sat and looked at the ancient animal. What a hunt. What a perfect hunt. The sun beat down on me then. And even as I sank into dreamy reflection, promising myself that I would return someday, I could have sworn I heard Robert Service.

"Why he left his home in the South to roam 'round the Pole, God only knows.
He was always cold but the land of gold seemed to hold him like a spell ..."

30

From pictures alone, one might view the arctic as only harsh and monotonous. But, according to the author, there is a unique beauty to this inhospitable land. The wondrous days like those from his second muskox hunt are all the more so when one has also witnessed the arctic's fury.

Chapter Three: Facing Down Fear

31

CHAPTER FOUR:
DIARY OF DESPAIR

March 1 — It's the first day of my polar bear hunt! Sort of. I'm on the first airplane segment of the trip. I'll be flying all night and most of tomorrow.

March 2 — Arrived safely today at 4 p.m. — with my Knight muzzleloader intact — at my final destination, Hall Beach, in the new Canadian territory of Nunavut. My good friend, Fred Webb, is the outfitter, and I met Ike Angotautok, the head guide and Daniel Kaunak the assistant guide. James Kukkik is the dog musher. From what I understand, James is already on the ice with the dog team.

March 3 — We're on the tundra! I got my polar bear tag at noon, and we headed out! We traveled as far as Hall Lake today and are staying at Daniel's father's tiny plywood shack tonight.

I've been riding on the back of the sled "komi-tick," pulled by a snow machine. "Rough" doesn't describe the ride, although it's still smoother than riding in my Pre-94 Mighty Dodge.

March 4 — Caught up with James today. It's been blizzarding for the past two days up here on the Melville Peninsula. James has been sitting in a canvas lean-to waiting out the storm. It's ugly out, zero visibility, but they say that we'll try to make it across to the Gulf of Boothia tomorrow. Didn't John Franklin and his crew disappear there? I think so. My fingers are cold, but crossed, and my hopes high. Tonight will be the first night in the canvas tent.

March 5 — Made it to the ice today! We hit saltwater at the mouth of Garry Bay. We set up the tent beside a small rocky island, right at the edge of the "rough ice." Not exactly what I expected, there ain't no going farther out into the Gulf; the bears will have to come to us. No open water and no seals. Just truck-sized slabs of ice jumbled up for as far as you can see. Why do I have an intense feeling of foreboding?

March 6 — First bear sighting! Today James and I traveled north on the dog sled nearly 15 miles. Temperature was approximately minus 35. As we searched for an opening in the rough ice, we spotted a sow and last year's cub! Unbelievable! We watched her for an hour and then set up camp for the night. James says that a boar will be following her.

March 7 — Evil luck today. James and I left camp early on the dogsled while Ike and Daniel lounged in the tent. At noon a monster 9-foot bear came right into camp and terrorized them! They had to shoot five times into the ice at its feet to make it back off. Even then it only backed up to 30 feet from the tent! The facts were written in the tracks.

By the time that James and I returned to camp, the bear was gone. Like I said, evil luck.

Ugly arctic weather is hard on man and beast. With luck, the author's first polar bear hunt could have ended in the first few days. Instead, it turned to weeks of struggle.

March 8 — Today was a day of rest. James thought that the bear might come back, so we stayed in camp. I glassed all morning and have apparently burned my eyeballs. My left eye is now snow-blind. It feels like someone first threw sand into it and then nails. It's going to take a couple days to heal, I think.

March 9 — We moved on today, James and I on the dogsled and the others on snow machine. We stopped after 10 or so miles and set up camp again. Low, blowing snow this morning, not too bad, about minus 30. As I write this, we're listening to the single side-band radio and the hissing of the tiny camp stove and Coleman lantern. These are the only sources of heat that we have, and we keep both going all night.

Now with my hunt past the halfway point, I think that it's time to recap the details.

Lunch is usually raw walrus, raw caribou or Mr. Noodle. Tonight we ate boiled walrus. Yesterday evening we had boiled caribou.

Having trouble with my bullets. The first two shots are totally haywire because of the sabot freezing and blowing apart, I believe. Now I'm trying to keep the gun warm on the dogsled by wrapping it in my sleeping bag and stuffing the bag full of disposable handwarmers. Thank you, Hot Hands!

There are 14 dogs in the team, four young pups and 10 adults. James uses a 30-foot whip, often, too often for my liking. I'm usually on my knees on the sled, and the fresh snow screeches, whines and complains as the sled drags over it. Probably travels about 3 or 4 miles an hour, I'd say. James yells directions to the lead dog in Inook.

So far we have only broken one snow machine. No problem, they roped the undercarriage together, and now it's fine.

The ice is extremely rough. Ten-foot-thick chunks, some the size of a house, stand on edge and sideways all stacked up and ugly. Under this jumble are ice cracks and seal holes. That's what the polar bears search for. So far we've only found a couple of seal holes, dens actually, where they make little caverns underneath the snow. They come up to breathe and then lay on the ice underneath the snow.

The lack of seal sign is disturbing. Not only does that mean that the polar bears won't be here, it means that we haven't had a chance to harpoon one for dog food yet. The dogs are already on half-rations. I suspect that we'll be next.

The idea, as I understand it, is to set up a base camp when we get to some place where there are lots of tracks and lots of bears and then we'll hunt from there in each direction. So far we're still looking. Haven't hit open water yet. Nights have been very clear.

The northern lights have been rare, only one night that I know of. Naturally one tries not to drink too much tea before bedtime; going out into the dangerous arctic night is a quick way to compromise one's chance of survival.

The moon is a silver sliver in the dark sky, and Ike tells me that when it's tipped on its side, like it is, it holds lots of animals. It's supposed to be a good time to hunt. At least that's what Inuit legend would have you believe. We'll see.

At certain times, late in the evening, the radio picks up sounds like some kind of weird music from China or Russia or something. We don't know. That's a sound that I've heard before in the western arctic. There they say that it's the ancestors singing.

I just counted and discovered that I have 19 different batteries in the pouch pocket of my overalls. I keep them there, even in my sleeping bag, to keep them warm and working.

I have every inch of me covered during the day on the dogsled and still have impressive black frost burns across by forehead and on my nose. James wears nothing on his face! Unbelievably, these guys don't appear to get cold.

A shower here in the arctic consists of a small tin can with a string on the top attached to a nail that hangs on the tent ridge pole, about four feet off the ice. There are holes cut into the can so you can fill it with hot water. Then you let it drip on you as you kneel under it on the ice. So far I haven't had a shower because I don't think that I smell. Everyone suggests that perhaps my nose isn't working properly.

We have gone through a 3-pound can of sugar so far.

I've learned that dog fur is the best for parkas and mukluks. It apparently doesn't frost up and is better than wolf or wolverine. Me thinks there isn't much of a future being a sled dog up here.

My toothpaste and toothbrush are frozen. Deodorant is a lot of fun to put on in the morning. However, since I don't smell, I don't use it.

Daniel sleeps with his gun right beside him. It's a .243 Winchester, so we're safe. Not!

I think James is starting to exhibit signs of … regressing? As we were coming back to camp on the sled last night, in the pitch dark, he was howling at the moon like a wolf!

In the tent and in my sleeping bag I wear long johns, a sweater and wool pants and jacket. I'm always cold unless I get into my sleeping bag or the guys crank the stove up. That doesn't happen very often as we're already running short of gas.

March 10 — It's been a day of mishaps, this our fifth day hunting on the ice.

We had a problem in the middle of the night because the stove went out. James pumped it up and was about to light it when he discovered that the white gas was leaking out and had filled up the bottom of the stove. We were probably within seconds of a huge flash fire. Close call.

Also, I fell up to my thighs in a seal den. Just missed falling into the water by inches. Close call.

Also fell off the dogsled and rammed both shins onto the edge of an ice block. Am now laying here gimped up with an ice pack on each shin. At least it's no problem finding ice up

The bear tracks in camp the third day of the hunt served as an evil reminder and were one of the rare sets of tracks that the crew encountered during the three-week hunt.

here. I just chip it from our floor. The lump on one shin is the size of a grapefruit, but it could have been worse. Last spring, a sport hunter got his fingers caught over the edge of the sled and sliced a couple of them off. The dogs pull slowly, but with incredible force.

It was bitter cold today, coldest day yet because of the wind—easily 70 or 80 below counting the wind chill.

Unbelievably, water isn't easy to come by up here. There's a lot of snow, but it takes too much of our gas to melt enough of it for coffee, so the guys go out and look for old "blue" freshwater icebergs. The ice under us is too salty to use for drinking.

Glassing for bears is nearly impossible in the cold. The instant that you lift your binos, they start fogging because your eyeballs are a little warmer than the binos are.

It was a beautiful red sunset this evening.

March 11—Everything froze during the
night. The juice jug froze solidly inside the tent.

My frostbite is getting worse. Apparently if you get it really bad your whole nose turns black and it falls off. Nice. There are three people in Hall Beach who have amputations because of frostbite. One old fellow lost both of his legs while walrus hunting. He was lucky.

His two hunting buddies froze to death.

Ike told us a true story about a local village. Apparently the hunters all left the village to go find something to eat. They were starving in the winter and left an old man in charge of all the women and children in the village. The old cannibal ate 19 of them before the hunters returned. Ike says that he's been there and seen all of the skulls. Interesting after-dinner-in-the-arctic conversation. I decided to keep my muzzleloader closer during the night.

I must be getting clumsier as I get more run-down from the constant cold. I fell off the sled again today; the whole thing tipped over on me. Close call.

Very disappointing, didn't find any fresh tracks today. No seals. No nothing.

We're down to the last meal of walrus. I'm sure that they'll be very upset once they run out.

Daniel told us a story about when he was 13 walking with his little brother and uncle on the ice near Hall Beach and they all fell in and only he survived.

Today was the toughest day on the dog sled. It just seemed to go on and on forever … slow, and right into the wind.

March 12—The seventh day of actual
hunting and again clear, beautiful skies. Aren't we lucky? The fire went out in the night, so my gun is frozen again. And as it thaws out, of course, the frost condenses into waterfalls down the barrel and then on to the powder. I'm going to have to change my powder again. This cold

weather is wreaking havoc on my equipment.

We actually camped in relative luxury tonight because we're on top of snow instead of ice. That meant that we could dig down about 14 inches to make a bed shelf for the sleeping bags. We can sit with our feet down; it's almost like sitting in a chair! Luxury is a relative thing up here.

Today the sled runners screeched when they crossed the snow. It was like listening to 1,000 people scratching their fingernails down a chalkboard for eight hours straight. Sometimes it sounds like tires squealing or dogs howling or banshees screaming.

Clear and cold today, but dismal as far as hunting goes. No tracks.

It's getting harder to stay positive.

My ski goggles have been fogging up about five minutes into the sled ride lately. Once they do, it's like living inside of a cage, just bumping around on the sled and you can't see at all, not even one inch past your face. It makes sitting on the sled all day even more brutal.

March 13 — Pretty well the "same-old, same-old" today. We headed back to where we camped on day two. It's depressing to go back to the same dead zone again.

March 14 — Nothing much happened today. Never saw a single track. Almost too depressing to even talk about. No doubt about it, depression has set in — blackness, a little hope, melancholy. We'll go onward, but it now looks pretty hopeless.

March 15 — It's morning. Ike is leaving to go back for supplies. However, I'm staying because I enjoy it out here in this brutal place. Right?

Last night we feasted on boiled arctic char — head, guts and all ...

Wow! A polar bear just came through our camp! Just when everything seemed so hopeless! Unfortunately, it was a small one. Twice it came in and twice they had to shoot their guns into the snow at its feet. Got some great video footage!

The few bears that the author saw during the hunt were sows or small boars. Any hope of success faded with each passing day.

Ultimate Big Game Adventures

March 16—This would now be 14 days on the ice. Ike should be near Hall Beach. Today we're sitting, not going anywhere, I guess. I'd have to say that we're getting low on most things at this point.

I'm supposed to be on the airplane today, going home.

No fresh tracks around camp last night. Nothing, no hope, and we're waiting. We'll see what happens.

I stood outside the tent today for a bit. It's absolutely desolate, ice all around. The ice is popping and groaning. Once in a while a crackling roar passes like a wave. I guess that the tides create a pressure edge, crushing the ice against itself.

What a forbidding place.

March 17—Clear day again. We didn't go hunting. Almost out of all food and supplies.

Before he left, Ike told a story about him finding a walrus way out on the rocky top of the Melville Peninsula last year. Apparently, when the walrus came onto the ice and the ice closed up behind him, the walrus decided to travel 200 miles to the other side of the peninsula. Funny, never thought I'd relate to a walrus, but somehow I think I know just how out of place he felt.

It could be worse. One could come back in the next life as a snowflake in the arctic—now that's hopeless.

Before he froze to death at the South Pole, Robert Falcon Scott wrote, "The borderline between necessity and luxury is vague enough." Now I know what he meant.

The moon tonight is almost seven-eighths and it's stunning. I put binoculars on it and could see the crater edges; it's so clear up here.

March 18—Day 16. The wind picked up today, gusting to 30 mph, maybe more. It was nasty, but we finally struck camp and moved on.

Had an unbelievable experience today. We were on the dogsled when we hit a fresh set of

A chance to smile amid the despair. This cub was 400 yards from its mother, who was preoccupied looking for seals.

sow and cub tracks. As we looked at the tracks, the dogs went nuts. Off on one side, only 400 yards away, the sow and cub were sniffing seal holes. On the other side, only a few yards away, a second tiny cub was headed for the dogs! James handled the dogs, and I picked up the cub and took it over to the other side of the sled. We snapped a couple of pictures and sent the cub on its way back to its mother! Last I saw they were all sniffing seal holes. It was wild.

We just heard that one of the two snow machines, on its way to re-supply us, broke down. We are going to drink the last little bit of coffee we have. Who knows what will happen tomorrow?

An Inuit guide hacks at the frozen walrus meat that sustains the men and the dogs.

We're not going anywhere today. Ike and Daniel are attempting to fix their two beat-up snow machines.

It's a cold morning, overcast with a little bit of wind shaking the tent. Got up at 6 as usual. James was up first, dipping instant coffee bags into boiling water. I had my usual three cups of bad coffee. What I wouldn't give for a strong cup of boiled cowboy coffee.

After all this time in this tiny, canvas tent, there's caribou hair in everything—coffee, soup, dinners, all from the hides that we lay on and from the caribou skin pants. The wind is getting worse. We couldn't go anywhere if we wanted to.

It's starting to drift, so we're waiting to see if there's a storm coming.

The wind is rising, 30 to 40 mph now with drifting snow. It's pretty nasty out there, bitter cold.

It's a blizzard.

March 20—The wind
has let up. Ike left for Hall Beach. He's left us with one tank of gas in the snow machine and five extra gallons in a can. Now we'll have to get re-supplied again! Barely two days after Ike brought us the last re-supply!

I don't think James is going to take his dogs anywhere, they've just about had it. Even with the two new dogs, the team is dragging poorly. I doubt that he's going to want to move out of this spot.

I think that James and Daniel are getting awfully tired of this, and that makes three of us.

March 21—I'm not sure what day it is,
Tuesday, I think, and I'm laying here. It's early, first thing in the morning. The other guys are still sleeping, and the tent is rattling and shak-

March 19—Day 17. Ike made it to us
late last night with only a small portion of the re-supply and two extra dogs to augment the pathetic creatures that we've been using. I believe they are starting to suffer beyond the call of duty. At least one is on its last legs. For me, it's difficult to watch. I have to force myself to remember that the rules of existence are different in the high arctic.

ing, and we're obviously in the middle of a blizzard. I guess there won't be any hunting today.

Breakfast was two cups of coffee and two peanut butter sandwiches. I heated the frozen bread over the lantern just to get it warm enough to spread the peanut butter on and eat it, no butter no nothing. No big deal. Outside the blizzard is raging.

It's around noon, and the blizzard is getting worse, you can just barely see the dogs that are only 30 or 40 feet from the tent.

The tent is taking a pounding as the wind beats on it. I'm not sure how hard the wind's blowing, but it's got to be about 40 miles an hour. It's deafening.

March 22 — Tuesday, I'm guessing … I don't know. It's about 9:30 a.m. We're having eggs in a bag this morning. They keep eggs up here by cracking them into a Zip-Loc bag. Then they let them freeze. To prepare them, you simply dump them into the frying pan and cook them.

Everything freezes up here, everything. I was a little cooler last night in my sleeping bag; it's getting damp. It's not blizzarding anymore, but it's bad, still snowing, whiteout conditions.

We're not going hunting today.

I'm having a cup of coffee and I'm looking in my mug and I can count 1-2-3-4-5-6-7-8-9-10-11-12-13 caribou hairs in my coffee. Mmmm good.

We're out of food again, almost; I ate Cheerios without milk or sugar for dinner.

March 23 — This is the 21st day on the ice and 23rd day of the trip.

James is pretty well done.

We got our re-supply late this evening, but I'm afraid that it's too little too late. Before our re-supply, we met up with another dog musher out on the ice—our first contact with another human! He'd killed a small polar bear yesterday and gave us some ribs. We boiled them up right then and there and ate them. Good, but somehow they left a bitter taste in my mouth. I guess it's because I've spent a lifetime dreaming about tasting my own polar bear!

March 24 — It's over. Twenty-two days … 24 since I left home. I think that we did our

It's not lobster, especially after eating it for 17 straight days!

best under the circumstances. With luck it would have been over way back on March 7 when the big bear walked into camp while James and I were a mile away.

Daniel and I want to use the next few days to hunt our way back south, but James won't go on, he can't, nor can the dogs; he's going home. He's already loading the sled. He's not even taking the tent. He's going to make an igloo every night until he gets back to Hall Beach in four days or so. Hopefully the dogs will make it. Daniel will pull me back on the komitick.

March 25 — It's 1 a.m., and Daniel and I just got back to Hall Beach after a grueling 12-hour ride. That's it. It's over; I didn't get a polar bear.

The worst thing is, I've got to go back out to that God-forsaken icy place and try again. ■

Chapter Five:

EPILOGUE: DANGER KNOCKS

Cape Dorset, Nunavut (One year later) ...

March 27, 2002 —It's not cold
exactly, minus 10 or 20, but hardly any wind.
I'm dressed for colder. It's absolutely stunning. The snow is brilliant with the sun shining on the white, and the rocks are pitch
black. The dogs are pulling fast and fresh.
We're off!

Bear! First day! Three hours from Cape Dorset,
and there's a polar bear standing about 400
yards away looking at us right now! We've just
come around to this flat ocean ice, and here's
this bear right out in the middle, about a 7-foot-
er, gorgeous. So primitive, so white. The bear
has run off and turned around and come back
part way and is sitting at the edge of the land
and the sea. Unbelievable. This is so spectacular. The sun's out, it's shimmering across this
beautiful, flat ice. Could this portend well for
the hunt? I hope.

Oh, God! We're still heading toward where
we're going to camp tonight, and I just saw a
polar bear that ... I never imagined anything
could be that big, it was huge! We came
around a peninsula, and there he was. He started moving away and couldn't even run
because he was so huge. I don't know how big
he was—just so big, my God, my God! I'm
shaking and I wasn't even close to him, I don't
even know if I want to get close to something
that big! On the other hand, I'd give just about
anything to get close to something that big! I
don't know how big he was ... 11 feet? 12 feet?
Bigger? I don't know.

We'll head over to check his tracks in a
minute. My three Inuit guides are up on a hill
looking across where the bear went out to the
open flow edge. So he's gone. I've been
spoiled already this first afternoon. Already
two bears, one small one and one, the largest
living creature I think I've ever seen.

It's dead still out here. The ice is cracking. I
see the rough ice out at the flow edge, it looks
like houses moving in the distance, but they're
actually icebergs in the open water. That's the
rough ice and where the big bear was headed
and no way to get him once he gets into that
crap. Gosh, he was big. If we're lucky, maybe
we'll see something that size, I don't know.
Pretty special just to lay eyes on such an animal.
I'm lucky to be out here.

The sun is setting now, the Inuit say it's a full

moon and that's why the animals are moving. Huh, just the opposite of down south. There are sun doggies on each side of the sun—cold, clear weather, I think. One guide, Pitsulak, is chopping up chunks of walrus to feed the dogs. They're fighting and whining all tied up in a line. My head guide, Nuna, is busy out by the sled, and the other guide is inside the igloo boiling some water.

It's dark now, and we've eaten boiled walrus and "Cup-of-Soup" mixed together. It actually makes for a good feed when it's boiled up like that. Nuna is on the single side-band radio talking to I'm not sure who; I can barely make him out. It's comforting listening to the sounds of the people across the whole arctic talking to each other, it doesn't matter how fuzzy or crackly sounding they are, it's like there are friends out there somewhere in the dark and white and cold. I'm lying inside my sleeping bag on a bed of furs, and we have two white gas burners going. It's almost comfortable. We're talking about the monster Nanook we saw today, hoping that he comes back to visit us tonight. They do, I don't.

March 28—Another brilliant, sunny day. I was tossing and turning all night. Lying on the snow, with not much for furs underneath me made for a little harder bed than what I'm used to. Outside the dogs are sleeping in the sun. There's a beautiful white arctic fox probably 50 yards away waiting for any scraps that the dogs might have missed. Good luck, Mr. Fox. Pitsulak is up on the hill right now looking for polar bears.

The dogs are pulling the sled on a fan trace, they're catching around the ice hummocks and knobs and hills, makes for one heck of a tangled mess, but somehow these guys just keep going through. Our progress has slowed. We've probably done 40 miles today, but the dogs are still going strong.

No luck on the polar bear so far, but we just stopped, and there are three wolves. Pitsulak shot the big, white male. I'm standing here right now with the snow drifting around on this sort of an inlet, with big rock islands on three sides around us and all three of my guides are bent over skinning the white wolf. There's a polar bear skeleton lying exposed on the windswept rocks. Nuna says that he killed the bear several months ago when it tried to crawl into his tent to eat him at 4 a.m.! Foreshadowing? I hope not.

March 29—Good Friday today!
It's morning. We're sitting in the igloo that we made last night. There's the hiss of the burner, and the single side-band radio is on. An Inuit country gospel chorus has commandeered the airwaves and is singing "Will the Circle be Broken" on the radio in an igloo somewhere out on the ice a couple days' dogsled travel from Cape Dorset! Puts the world in a unique perspective.

The sun shines through the walls of the igloo, and it has occurred to me that snow grows like trees. Snow has age rings here, or at least storm rings. The snow in this area looks to be 25 storms deep. You can count the storms. It storms, snow falls and when it stops snowing, ice fog rolls in and puts a layer of ice on the

Building an igloo requires master craftsmanship. Inside, on a bed of caribou hides, it sleeps like the Hilton ... almost. Ancient Inuit legend about this particular igloo suggested good things to come.

fresh snow. This has happened 25 times since last summer. It's quite pretty. The sun shines through the ice much easier than the layers of snow, so the lines of ice are easily counted.

I'm impressed with the good humor of these Inuit hunters. If they trip and fall and smack down onto the ice, they turn over smiling and laughing. One was sitting in the igloo when one of the chunks of snow melted off and fell on his head. It was a good 40-pound chunk of snow that put out the burner; there was snow everywhere, on all the food. You'd think that they'd be upset, but they laughed until they were nearly crying!

There must be wolves in the area early this morning. Right at first light our dog team started howling just like a pack of wolves or coyotes would do, yipping and yiping. My guides believe that the dogs must have heard a wolf pack howling in the distance and were answering. I don't think that it would take much to put these sled dogs right back into their wild state. In fact, I'm quite positive that they're wilder than they are tame.

I'm outside now, and the sun is very bright; I can feel my eyes burning even inside my tinted goggles. I can barely take my goggles off for more than a minute. My eyes start to water and it's pretty painful. Have to watch out for snow blindness. As we break camp and load the sleds, I notice that this spot between two big

islands has obviously been used as an Inuit camping spot for ages. There are old pieces of sled runners, and you can see tent rings.

This is a spectacular part of the world right here. Apparently, 100 years ago there was a sailing ship that got trapped in the ice of the bay right around the corner from us. The sailors built themselves a little bit of shelter with the rocks and spent the whole winter nearby. I'll have to look that up and find out what ship it was. The Franklin expedition?

We traveled hard today and have made camp. Our new igloo is done, just had our tea and they've used an axe to chop up the frozen raw walrus chunks for the dogs. I'd say 2 to 3 pounds is the per-dog ration. Pitsulak and I grabbed all of the smaller scraps off of the snow and wolfed those down. We're chopping

a bit more off because that's what we'll eat for dinner tonight — boiled walrus. Once walrus is boiled, it's a lot better than when it's raw.

Good Friday dinner is over; we're sitting here listening to the static on the radio and the hiss of the burner. It's a bigger igloo tonight, lots of room, 10 feet across I'd say. We had no plates, so we just ate the walrus out of a communal pot. Cut and chew. The doorway is blocked with a slab of snow. We're trapped inside … we're close to our hunting area. Nuna is excited suddenly. He's pointing at the igloo wall at five snow blocks that align vertically. They're explaining to me that it's a folklore thing, very rare. The snow blocks are supposed to be offset like bricks. Five aligned like this is apparently a big deal because it means that the bear will come from that direction.

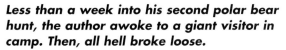
Less than a week into his second polar bear hunt, the author awoke to a giant visitor in camp. Then, all hell broke loose.

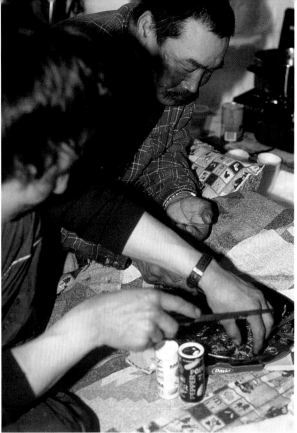

That direction is south. The flow edge is south.

March 30 — It's 6:30 a.m., and I'm lying here in my sleeping bag looking at the light filtering through the various cracks in the igloo wall. The sun must be poking over the horizon. Nuna and one of the guides are talking quietly in Inuit, and the kettle is steaming. The dogs are yipping and yakking and fighting and growling as usual, but now, suddenly, they've stopped. We listen. One is growling in a low pitch. We all hear it. It's a warning! Something is close, something big. Pandemonium!

All of us are fighting our way out of our sleeping bags, and the Inuit are yelling "Nanook, Nanook!" We can't see outside, we're totally blocked off inside this igloo; even the door is blocked off with a slab of snow. Nuna's grabbing for the saw and stabbing it through the side of the igloo, frantically cutting and yelling "Nanook! Nanook!" Everybody has his own agenda.

Nuna has cut a hole through the wall and is

looking to the south. He sees something! I'm grabbing for my Knight muzzleloader and possibles bag. I don't know what's going on except that everyone is frantic around me. Nuna's looking out the hole that he cut and yelling for me to "Shoot! Shoot!" Now he's pushing by me and stabbing the saw through another spot in the wall. The bear is obviously passing by the igloo!

Suddenly all of them are on the far side of the igloo, and they grab me and pull me over to that side. A huge shadow crosses right beside the igloo where I'd just been trying to load my gun! They're worried that the bear is going to pound his way into the igloo to get us! Like rats in a trap! But now the shadow has passed and is heading toward the dogs, and Nuna's stabbing the saw through the side of the igloo again, cutting and cutting and then punching his fist through the cut out section and looking quickly and then pointing. "Nanook! Nanook!"

The bear swatted at one of the tethered dogs, the dogs are going nuts. I'm loading, I can see through the hole that Nuna has cut. Now the bear is crossing to the front of the igloo. Now that shooting hole is no good. Nuna's cutting out another triangular window. The bear is at the sled, and for the first time now I see how

really huge it is. Nuna's yelling for me to "Shoot!" But even though my muzzleloader is loaded now, I'd have to shoot the bear right in the head. He's 15 feet away at most and eating walrus from out of the sled—the same walrus that we had for supper last night.

Pitsulak is thinking the most clearly right now and has grabbed my camera and hands it to me. I take pictures through the cut window! I can see the bear's head, so close and so huge! A scarred, big giant with yellowed teeth; this animal is an old warrior, the survivor of the cruelest winters this planet has to offer. He's survived a lifetime of brutality. I decide that I can't shoot or really that I won't shoot. Not through this hole. It wouldn't be right to snipe him. This magnificent animal deserves better. I shake my head and try to explain to Nuna. He stares at me, but understands. He turns and kicks out the block of snow that has blocked our doorway for the night. I crawl out.

The bear is 15 feet away eating and staring at me. It lifts its massive head now and, suddenly, I'm inspired by Pitsulak's quick thinking with the still camera. It occurs to me that I'm in the arctic to film an episode for my new television show. So I take 10 dangerous steps and grab the video camera from the other sled and bring it back inside the igloo. I open the case and pull out the camera, offering it to anyone. Pitsulak is the only one to reach out and take the camera.

I turn and step out again. I'm still in my stocking feet. Pitsulak follows me and begins video-taping. I step toward the bear trying to get an angle; two Inuit faces are beside me, sticking out of the igloo windows are yelling, "Shoot!" But I can't shoot, not from this angle. I'm too close to the bear to risk taking the shot. I work around the bear, but it turns to face me! He won't turn sideways to give me a shot at his heart or lungs. I make a decision. When the bear puts his head down for a second, I aim above the skull, at the base of the neck and pull the trigger. BOOM!

The bear drops in his tracks stunned, not enough power to break the neck bone?!! I'm reloading and everyone is running around congratulating me, but I know better. This bear is stunned, not dead. The bear starts to roll! He's starting to rise! Loaded, cap on, lift and shoot. BOOM! Smoke again. This time the bear is done. It's over! They're all yelling! Hands high, arms spread wide. Smiles all around. So big and so close, so unbelievably close. The bear is huge, a legitimate 10-footer!

It happened so quickly and just like the folklore said it would! The bear came from the south. It was hunting us in our camp. It was the king of this land. My Inuit are on the radio already. "Nanook! They caught the polar bear, the big one…!"

The hunt is over now. All that remains is heading back. My Inuit guides are outside the igloo making busy. We haven't begun to skin the bear yet, and I have a moment to reflect inside this igloo. This must be nearly as it was 3,000 years ago when the first Paleo-Eskimo hunters migrated across the land bridge from Siberia—these people Nuna, Pitsulak, these hunters, they live here still in this snow and cold. The snow they turn into beautiful sculpted round homes with a spiraling construction, homes that light shines through. They and animals like the polar bear living here and hunting each other … it puts into perspective what it means to be a hunter. This must be the way it is meant to be. ■

The author with his polar bear after nearly a month of trying. Two shots from the Knight muzzleloader stopped the 10-footer.

CHAPTER SIX:

COME HELL OR HIGH WATER

Destruction Island, Desolation Sound, Cape of Storms ... my finger stopped on the map when it touched Winter Harbor. There. Just outside the mouth of the harbor, off to one side, lay a tiny, remote inlet. That's where I'd find my record-book black bear and that's where I intended to hunt during the spring bear season ... come hell or high water.

The storm-poisoned sky turned the far end of the inlet black. We were only halfway across. I twisted the throttle harder, trying to coax another horse or two from the 7-horse Honda outboard. It didn't help. My knuckles were already white from twisting, but it felt better than watching helplessly as the squall pounded down the inlet toward us. Within seconds, the first waves began lifting from the calm surface, slapping a warning against the bow of our 10-foot aluminum boat. Then came the first raindrops and the first tentative puffs of wind; each testing our resolve to continue.

We had no choice but to continue across the open water. To go back would take as long as pressing onward. And in forward, at least, we'd be bashing the waves head-on. My partner sitting in the front of the boat turned his back to the approaching dark shadow. Not only was he at the mercy of the storm, but he was also at the mercy of my seamanship; no doubt he turned to watch my face for signs of fear. I don't think that I did much for his confidence when I reached down with my free hand and tightened the straps on my floater jacket.

The squall hammered us a minute later. Huge waves towered around us, their white tops whipped into a salty froth by the wind. The rain deluged now, drenching us and making it virtually impossible to see where we were headed. Not that it mattered. As long as we stayed headed into the teeth of the storm, we'd end up where we ended up. Staying afloat was all that counted. I lifted my free hand to give a thumbs-up to my hunting partner. That's when the motor sputtered and quit.

Nightmare? Unfortunately not. There was no waking up from this one.

BEAUTY BELIES DANGER

This happened in the spring of 1993. My hunting partner and I were hunting the northwest coast of British Columbia's Vancouver Island—an area that might have more and larger bears per square mile than any other part of the world. It's remote, with massive rainforested mountains rising steeply from the ocean shores.

51

Here and there along the northwestern coast, as though cut by the sword of some ancient God, the island interior is penetrated by deep, narrow inlets like the one we were crossing. There are few areas on this continent so breathtakingly beautiful or, for that matter, so breathtakingly dangerous. Many are the seamen who would tell you of the rainforested beauty of the rugged coastline. But there are many more lying quiet and cold forever, who would warn you of the unseen danger.

Hunting so close to the open ocean, one has almost no warning when storms, with nothing to do between Japan and North America but grow ugly, hit the coast with a vengeance. One minute all is calm. The next, one of these storms barrels around the corner of a mountain and all hell breaks loose. And that's on inside waters within the relatively protected confines of the deep fjords and inlets. The fury of these storms hitting the shoreline on the outside waters has to be seen to be believed.

Fortunately for us, our small craft never really had a chance to take any waves broadside. So urgent was my pull on the starter cord that the engine fired up again immediately and we con-

tinued holding our own. A lifetime later, the squall passed, leaving us to breathe freer and leaving the inlet surface chopped as a reminder of its passing. The bottom of the boat lay inches deep in saltwater, but there was little point in bailing. We were close to shore by then. We'd made it.

Only at that point did the stress that we'd both felt during the last few minutes manifest itself. As I pushed the kill button and turned to tilt the engine leg from the water, I felt the boat lurch violently. When I turned back to see what new menace was after us, I noticed immediately that my partner was gone. Or almost gone. His hand was hanging onto the side of the boat. The rest of him was under water. He'd been in such a hurry to get out of the boat and get his feet onto dry land, he hadn't remembered to wait until we reached the shallows.

It wasn't until several hours later, after we dried out, stopped shivering and sat by the campfire with a cupful of hot coffee, that we began to laugh nervously about the adventure. We both knew that it could've been much more serious — probably deadly serious if we'd headed out into the

open ocean like we'd originally planned earlier in the day. We'd almost attempted to cross to the remote inlet, the spot that I'd picked from a map months before and the spot that I'd vowed to hunt come hell or high water. Only at the last second, after we both got a bad feeling about the weather's intentions, had we changed our minds and decided to hunt the far side of the relatively sheltered inlet that we were camped on.

It hadn't been an easy decision to make. My heart was set on hunting the far inlet, and we'd already waited three shore-bound days for a break in the weather. When the weather finally did calm and it appeared that we might have a chance to make the five-mile ocean crossing to the mouth of the inlet, I'd almost let my desire influence my common sense. If we'd been caught by the same squall outside the harbor, we'd both be dead. Simple as that. The first bear hunters to visit Davey Jones' locker.

BEAR ISLAND

In fact, if getting a bear was my only intention, there wasn't really any need to risk the crossing to the remote inlet. I could've found unbelievable spring black bear hunting anywhere on northwestern Vancouver Island. This I knew from personal hunting experience and from my experience working as a guide for Wayne Wiebe, local bear hunting legend. Wayne founded Pacific Rim Guide Outfitters and at one time owned the hunting rights to most of the northern two-thirds of Vancouver Island. For more than a decade, clients of Pacific Rim Outfitters have been spotting, stalking and killing record-class black bears so consistently that northwestern Vancouver Island has become world famous.

Those bears, some 13,000 strong on the 12,000-square-mile island, head for the closest patch of green grass when they first wake up from their winter hibernation. Experience dictates that Pacific Rim's clients can reasonably expect to see 10 to 20 black bears per day any time during the season, which runs from April 1 through June 15. Baiting is illegal. All hunts are spot-and-stalk.

The largest of the bears, by nature, head for the best feeding areas; best being the places with the

Vancouver Island black bears are plentiful and some of the largest in North America.

most grass, most often located at river mouths or on the tidal flats found at the back end of most inlets. As often as not, an old boar, feeding on one of these flats, will have been doing so for years. Younger bears learn quickly to keep off the flat during prime time, and fights between contenders for the best feeding spots are common. Seldom does one kill a large bear without the scars of serious combat marring its face.

After the adventure with the squall, I decided that I could use some advice. So, after breaking camp and returning to civilization the next day, I called Wayne. He confirmed that the crossing to the inlet that I'd intended to hunt was certainly treacherous and that he wouldn't try to make it in weather conditions that were less than perfect. Rather than dampen my resolve to make it to the inlet, he tempered it when he told me that he'd never hunted that spot. Thus, he said, a record-book bear likely lived there.

AN OCEAN AWAY

That was enough for me. After a week's worth of work crammed into three days, I climbed into my 4-wheel-drive and headed back to the inlet.

The eight-hour drive in bright April sunshine raised my hopes that the coming week would bring calm, clear weather. I was determined to reach the inlet, but did not, under any circumstances, intend to risk life and limb like I had on the first aborted hunt.

My father-in-law came along this time, since my former hunting partner decided that he was just too busy to come up again ... ever. It was dark by the time we pulled into the camping spot and it was still dark when I awoke the next morning—an hour after what should have been first light. One look outside confirmed what I hoped was not true. Ugly black clouds scudded across the sky. Straight from Japan, they boded nothing but ill for any ideas I might entertain about crossing the open ocean to the remote inlet.

For three days we waited, and for three days storm after storm buffeted the coast. After the third day of waiting, we decided to call it quits until the following week. Even though we both would have loved to stay and eat more crabs, oysters, mussels and clams, we both knew that there was little chance of the weather clearing within the coming few days.

Biding his time, the author finally got the break in the weather that he needed to make a mad dash to the secluded inlet that held the black bear of his dreams.

So we broke camp regretfully and headed out, beaten by the weather for the second week in a row. Only a hunter can know the disappointment. For months before the season, I'd planned the hunt, settling eventually on what I considered to be the best area and then, more specifically, the best spot within that area. I'd allowed for everything, including extra time, but there was no way of predicting April weather that the old-timers said was the worst that they'd seen during their salty lifetimes.

Still, prepared for any contingency, I'd allowed myself one extra week of spring hunting time. Actually, I made a deal with myself to make up the lost week of work during the fall whitetail season. So again, after putting a week's worth of work into three days, I headed, by myself this time, back up to the north end of the island. And, once again, I awoke to find the whole coast socked in.

This time the thought of fresh seafood and incredible scenery did little to soften my mood. Nor did the simple option of seeing and stalking a big bear on one of the mountainsides accessible by 4x4, do much to brighten the day. I wanted to get around to the remote inlet by boat and I wanted to shoot my bear there. Any other hunt would not do, and a bear taken any other way wouldn't compare to taking one from the inlet by boat, no matter how big that bear might be. I wanted the hunt to be exactly

what I'd spent months imagining it would be.

IT'S GO TIME

For three days I waited for a break in the weather that didn't come. With two days left to hunt, I awoke to pouring rain and gale-force winds. It was obvious that there wasn't a hope for clear weather. A few quick calculations later and I knew what I had to do. Pack up and leave. If I did, I could work for a couple of days and be back in three. If I drove all night, that is. Two hours later I had my camp in the back of my truck and was about to load my boat on the rack when the oddest thing happened.

The wind stopped.

It wasn't until I looked up at the clouds hanging motionless above me that I really believed that the wind had died. Better yet, one small ray of sunlight broke through the clouds lighting up the far side of the inlet that I was camped upon. Before the steam started rising from the damp shoreline, I'd made up my mind. Time to cross.

There was no time to second-guess my decision. It was now or never. Within five minutes I was at full throttle, do-or-dying it toward the mouth of the harbor. Aware of the danger, I'd left a note on the seat of my truck for the old crab fisherman who'd been visiting my camp each day. I took some comfort in the thought that he'd be aware of my attempt to cross and, in a pinch, would come and pick me off the shore if I shipwrecked.

It took all the willpower that I could muster to make myself round the corner and face the ocean swells with nothing between us but the thin aluminum skin of the 10-foot boat. I was frightened. Even though the boat lifted up and down on each swell like a cork, my stomach knotted with inexplicable foreboding. The same swell, on some friendly spot along the coast would have been a piece of cake; there was no tangible reason for fear. Right. Just like standing on the edge of a skyscraper roof without a guard rail. Nothing to fear there either, except that the stakes are life and death. Thinking back now, I suppose that I was experiencing the equivalent of a bad case of vertigo.

Why would I choose to hunt the remote inlet in the first place? Was it the thought of huge bears? Not really. I suppose, being honest with myself, I knew that it would end up being a solo trip into personally uncharted territory; a challenge to my self-control and ability to stand at the edge of the skyscraper roof and look down. I knew that there'd be some hardship and some measured amount of danger in the fact that there'd be no guard rail, no safety net. But I also knew, if I succeeded, even if all I managed to do was make it to the inlet and back, I would have attained a personal goal.

Maybe "why" matters now. But then, as I willed the boat fast across the open water, nothing mattered except reaching the inlet—an inlet that seemed to be farther away than it should have been. It wasn't until I rounded the last set of razor-sharp underwater rocks that the crab fisherman had warned me about, that it sunk in. I'd done it. I was in the small inlet.

The tide was out by then, leaving the inlet a waterless, mud flat. Hidden clams of every size and description squirted saltwater fountains skyward.

Aware that it was a foot hunt from that point onward, I beached my small boat at the edge of the only deep spot and pulled it up to the high-water mark. Only at that point did I turn to take a close look up the inlet. The mud flat extended nearly half a mile back into the inlet and then gave way to a beautiful grass flat that a bear hunter only dreams of finding. Several hundred yards wide and the same distance long, the knee-high grass waved gently in the breeze. Blue cloudless sky by now stretched as far as the eye could see, and the intense beating sun turned the inlet into a shimmering, surreal place of steam and heat waves.

There! Directly across the inlet, at the edge of the

grass stood the bear that I knew would be there. No need for a second look, it was him. His paws pointed inward and he made every step look determined. Even from my distant vantage, his scarred face looked old.

Knowing that the old boar might only feed for a few minutes, especially with the hot sun beating on his jet-black fur, I grabbed my Knight muzzleloader and daypack from the boat. The wind was perfect. All I had to do was approach directly across the wind, staying low, below the level of the grass and I'd find myself within 100 yards of the bruin.

Yet, I found out quickly just how impossible my planned stalk would be. Fifty yards into the mud flat, my leg disappeared to the knee in gooey sludge. Quicksand! Later I learned that in spots this centuries-deep accumulation of flotsam can be 10 feet deep.

Forced to make a quick retreat, I had to change from a direct stalk to a serpentine attack. Working my way as far as I dared to go up the inlet, without having the wind carry my scent to the bear, I eventually found enough hard gravelly ground to make the crossing. Heading back along the far shore, duck-walking most of the way, I was, within 30 minutes, close to where I'd originally planned to be. Unfortunately, the bear wasn't.

During my head-down stalk, he'd fed back past me to the edge of the timber ready to call it a day. Realizing that the bear was more than 150 yards away—the extreme edge of my shooting range—I moved in. Dropping my daypack, I belly-crawled 50 yards toward the boar in world-record time. Fast though I might have been, quiet I obviously was not. When I looked up, his beady eyes were fixed on me.

It's doubtful that he'd ever seen a human before, and it's certain that he wasn't afraid of me. But his belly was full, and he was hot, and I suppose that he just decided that I wasn't worthy of a good thumping. He turned his massive body and slowly started toward the timber. I sat, anchored my elbows on my knees, slipped the safety off and waited for a shot. He was moving slowly, but I had no intention of taking the shot until he stopped. If he didn't stop, he'd live.

He was right at the edge of the timber when he decided to take one last look. The crosshairs settled behind his shoulder, and the muzzleloader bucked. The 310-grain slug fully penetrated his 450-pound body, and he was dead within 25 yards. When I walked up to him, it was obvious that he'd square more than 7 feet and make the top five in the blackpowder record book.

Happy? You bet. But even as I pulled out my camera to take a few pictures, I felt the fingers of vertigo. My hunt was only half over. A quick glance heavenward set my skin to crawling. The sun was just showing through the grey overcast. Over the hills at the oceanward end of the inlet, the first telltale clumps of cloud appeared. But worse, by far, was the booming sound of distant surf and the stiffening breeze.

THE RACE FOR HOME

With the skinning and quartering done, I double-timed it back to the boat, careful to backtrack exactly my original stalk. I had shivering visions of sinking to my belly in quicksand. Then, trapped, I'd be tortured as the tide eased in over my head. Luckily when I reached the boat, this pleasant thought was replaced with one of drowning and being dashed to bits on the rocks by the pounding surf.

Weighted down as I was with the bear, the tiny boat barely seemed to move. Out the mouth of the inlet and around the rocks, I kept my thoughts focused on the task at hand. There were white-caps starting to appear when I hit the open ocean.

The swells were already swollen and choppy. The boat bucked this way and that, sliding break-neck into the valley of one swell and then slowing to a stop as it tried to climb up the back of the next. The first drops of rain stung my face. I risked a look behind. The black turbulent storm front closed the gap. But rather than feel fear at the sight, I felt safe for the first time in hours. There smashing through the swells, headed toward me, no doubt seeking safe harbor, were two large trawlers. There was no doubt that they could see me bobbing up and down and no doubt that they'd come to my aid should I founder.

Suddenly, the waves seemed smaller. I'd been in worse closer to home in friendly waters. As long as I was careful, I'd make it without much more than a few gray hairs to show for my efforts. The two boats were my safety net, the railing around the roof of a skyscraper. My vertigo vanished.

I made it back to my campsite safe and sound

Finding the largest big game animals is often a matter of finding remote areas that receive little hunting pressure. For the author, that approach paid off.

with a record-book black bear that green-scored 20⅝ Boone and Crockett inches. I'd hunted him exactly as I'd dreamed.

I was looking at a map the other day and found another inlet, even more remote. This one's impossible to reach by boat, but there's this logging road about a day's walk away. I figure if a guy used a compass to find his way and he didn't lose his cool in the primal tangled jungle, and didn't mind do-or-dying it to the edge of the unknown, there just might be a record-book bear waiting for him there. ∎

CHAPTER SEVEN:

ON THE TRA
OF DANGER

Dawn at the best of times rises gently out of the night, unfurling like a morning flower to light a dark world. If you're a hunter, you will have seen this dawn and know it for a time of quietude, a time of respectful silence, a time just before first light when no animal moves out of reverence for the beginning of the new day. Dawn at the best of times is a whispered promise.

But there's another dawn. This dawn crawls out of the night like an evil omen. It slides slowly across the land, sinister and bloated with a fog that turns black to grey and promises nothing but ill. This dawn the hunter will know well, too, for this is the dawn of damp cold and shivering apprehension.

I hunched my shoulders against the mist, trying to block the damp from seeping farther down the back of my shirt. The fog bumped and swirled around me, set to motion by the tiny movement that I'd made.

It was a warning. Be still intruder.

The water flowed silently over the flat, brown rocks delivering itself to the ocean only a half-mile away. A salmon flopped on the surface, frightening another which rocketed up the river, a watery swell over its humped back. I hid leaning against a cut bank, standing in a pool to my knees. At my feet a dozen more salmon prepared nests by laying on their sides and flailing into the gravel with their tails.

At the bottom of the pool a dozen more salmon finned quietly awaiting the slow, malignant death of the leper. They were done breeding, done living. Their fins were white and rotting, and their once sleek, silver sides were now mottled with horrible black sores. Every 15

In fall, coastal bears become salmon-eating machines. When the salmon run is on, bears concentrate on the rivers and streams.

minutes it seemed, one of these grotesque creatures would turn sideways to the current, give up and die; leaving the current to deliver it much the way its life began.

Though I couldn't see far enough upstream through the fog to confirm it, the lifeless carcasses floating past me told of thousands of salmon breeding and dying in the pools upstream. Probably it was the morbidity of that knowledge, life begetting death, begetting life, begetting death that made the fog seem like it was hanging heavily around me like a sinister foreshadowing pall.

SALMON MEAN BEARS

I waited another apprehensive hour in the fog and then for the first time since I'd waded up the creek from the ocean, I shifted my feet and prepared to move. It was time. The dawn gave ground to daylight. The fog had lifted to hang in the branches of the ancient trees leaning over the stream, and I could see well enough to hunt. Long fingers of seafoam green Spanish moss hung through the gauzy layer of fog, brushing my face and sending creepy shivers down my spine.

Slowly I advanced upstream, one tentative searching step at a time. I moved slowly both to make sure of my footing on the slippery algae-covered rocks and to make sure that I didn't break the eerie silence by splashing.

God knows I wanted to run, to charge ahead and meet the future. The strain of not knowing what the next second could bring was nearly too much to handle. I wanted the showdown to begin and the results known. It wasn't because I was confident of the outcome. I wasn't. And it wasn't because I wanted to be somewhere else. I didn't. It was more like I knew there was no escaping the inevitable, so why not get it over with?

I was hunting black bears. Not just any black bear mind you, but a big, old brute—the winner of a long lifetime of fighting for survival in the formidable old-growth rainforests of Vancouver Island. It was early fall, the time when the biggest of the bears pad furtive along each and every salmon stream cutting into the shoreline of the rugged West Coast of North America. Along many salmon streams, like the one that I was hunting, the bear trails are worn several inches deep, testament to 10,000 years of use.

Every fall, like clockwork, these secretive and savvy animals return to these streams to take advantage of the various salmon runs, feeding on the fat-rich fish. Between runs, these same bears retire to mountainside berry patches, partaking of the bounty to be had there. Whether these mighty animals are on the streams or in the berry patches, they are for the most part safe from hunters. You see, most hunters have black bears filed under "spring activity" or "bait hunting" or, even worse, "unworthy."

That's a shame.

Hunting black bears during the fall, by stalking, is one of the ultimate hunting experiences this continent offers, and the hunter who denies himself the opportunity to experience this type of hunt, for whatever reason, is an unfortunate soul, indeed. Baited hunts can't hold a candle.

Perhaps it's because when bait is used, the hunter is positioned safe and sound in a tree at a precise distance from the bait. On a baited black bear hunt, too, careful planning negates most other factors. That type of hunt, as any baited hunt must be, is too predictable. Not that there's anything wrong with that, there isn't ... if you like predictable.

Bears can be feeding on salmon one second and in the security of the rainforest jungle the second.

Chapter Seven: On The Trail Of Danger

Stalking along a Vancouver Island salmon stream requires the hunter to be constantly on his toes.

I stopped mid-step, searching with every fiber for the origin of the sound. I wasn't sure where it came from, but it was a sound. For sure it was a sound.

Suddenly, the whole world erupted above my head. I cowered and ducked from the blast, jumping to the side, my mouth frozen in a silent curse. What the ... ?!

An eagle, bald but immature, jumped from a branch stretching across the stream 10 feet above my head. Its wings spread 6 feet across at least. In the dead quiet of the morning, its take-off thundered.

After several minutes, my heart rate settled to only slightly accelerated. I knew that I was too nerved up to hunt effectively. It's often like that when you hunt black bears during the fall. So, I waited and gathered myself.

Black bears are just as dangerous as most hunters dangerously underestimate them. Once you've hunted them on the ground and on their terms you understand. Two years before, one of my guides had been mauled by a black bear that a client had wounded. Every year we face problem bruins and the inescapable danger.

A salmon splashed several yards away in a deep pool and a raven croaked somewhere out of sight downstream. The eagle's flight seemed to have awakened the morning. A smaller bird started singing in mellifluous contrast to the raven. Another salmon jumped close by.

There! One second the stream ahead was undisturbed. The next, it was a stream with a huge, black leg stepping into it. A bear! And a big one by the looks of its leg. I couldn't see anything above the bear's elbow because a dead snag 50 yards ahead obscured my vision. The bear might have been another 10 yards past the tree, but I couldn't be sure.

Seconds later, more of the bear's body emerged from the jungle. My heart hammered, and I breathed unevenly. The morning had already strained my nerves. Now I faced the showdown that had lured me here.

The bear couldn't have seen me any better than I could see him, but I had the advantage. He was

STALKING IN THE RIVER JUNGLE

None of this, of course, was going through my mind as I peered into the gloom upstream. As I still-hunted, I shifted my Knight muzzleloader from hand to hand in order to move the hanging moss strands away from my face and out of my line of sight. At each bend in the stream, I'd slow even more and lean ahead ever so carefully to peer around the corner. Every time, my heart would roar to full throttle.

The remains of the ominous dawn still clung here and there to the darker stretches of the stream. But, by now, the first rays of sun dappled the highest treetops. It was colder by a measure than it had been earlier, but I sweated a cold, clammy, fearful sweat.

Something bumped my hip wader and I startled. My heart pounded uncontrollably, disregarding the message my wide eyes relayed—just a dead salmon.

What was that?!

This bear emerged from the forest just 60 yards from the author. Though the bear spotted him, the author was ready.

moving. I was still. He stepped from the bank and waded to an exposed gravel bar mid-stream. The ocean tide had been receding all morning, dropping the stream level. The bear knew this and came to feed on the corpses of any salmon caught in the riffles along the gravel bar. He'd probably been feeding that way undisturbed for most of his 15 years. He had no reason to expect a hunter to be there, especially in the fall.

But I was there.

They say that a bear's sight is poor, and that is true. But when that old boar stepped into the open around the broken trunk of that overhanging snag, he glared my way instantaneously.

He didn't run, and I didn't rush my shot. We both knew the score. ∎

CHAPTER EIGHT:

OL' THREE LEGS

You might not believe this story, but I'll tell you it anyway. Once upon a time in a remote fishing village along British Columbia's coast, I was walking along a dilapidated boardwalk at the ocean's edge. The boardwalk connected the 10 or so houses that made up the village and, for all intents and purposes, served as the main street. I knew that I was in bear country because I'd seen a small bear eating greenery in the front yard of one of the houses as I walked past. I watched the bear eat dandelions until he saw me and bolted.

The next house had a dock stretching out into the ocean, and there was this old fisherman working on a boat. Naturally I stopped to talk to him about bears. I was hunting and wondered if he might have seen any bears around besides the one next door.

"Old what?" I asked, stopping the crusty gent part way into his answer.

"Old Three Legs," he repeated before continuing with his story. "Old Three Legs has been showing up on these here shores for ages. Aye, comes down in the storms, he does."

The old pirate, I mean fisherman, looked up toward the sky when he said "storms" and then lowered his gaze to fix me right in the eye, daring me to doubt him. I didn't, and he continued.

"Tried for him myself, I did," he said. He pointed down the shoreline to where it disappeared around the corner of the inlet. "Had him cold to rights, too. Came right in on him with my darlin' Betsy Lee. Bobbing and popping like spit on a grill, she was. Damn near put her on the rocks. Old Three Legs didn't pay no attention, though. He jes kep' on eatin' like me and Betsy Lee didn't exist. God rest her sweet yard arm."

The old fellow took a moment's silence. I noticed that the boat he was working on was called the Betsy Lee II.

"Managed to get a shot off, too," he continued. "Direct hit. Swear to it." The pirate lowered his voice. "Know what Old Three Legs did?"

"Died?" I assumed.

"Died!?" The old pirate lifted his head and cackled. "Died? Why you can't kill Old Three Legs, son! Vanished, he did. Just like that."

He snapped his dirty fingers and turned around to crawl back below decks. He cackled all the way down into her dieskly depths. Feeling like an idiot, I turned to walk back down the dock. In the distance I heard his echoing voice waft up from Betsy Lee II's

bowels. "Comes in on the storm, he does."

Sounds weird, right? Unbelievable and strange, too, right? I agree, but I was there. Granted, I might have dramatized the accent, and maybe he wasn't quite as cryptic as I remember, but I swear on a stack of muzzle-loading magazines that everything else is exactly as I remember—three-legged bear and all.

It gets stranger.

THE STORM STRIKES

Exactly three weeks later I was hunting by myself. I'd taken a 20⅝-inch bear a few days before and aimed to fill my second tag. The old man was a distant memory. When I stopped my truck at the edge of the inlet, several miles from the fishing village, I almost decided to forget hunting for the evening. Nasty black, billowing clouds boded ill for anyone venturing out in a boat. Besides my boat being only 10 feet long, I was hunting with my Knight muzzleloader. Rain and blackpowder don't mix.

I wrestled with my lazy self before deciding that I was there to hunt, so hunt I should. By the time I pulled the boat from the back of my truck, dragged it to the water and loaded it with my gear, the storm raged. Luckily the inlet was well protected and narrow.

I ducked my head against the pelting rain and started toward the back of the inlet. The rain pounded so hard that it was difficult to see much more than a couple hundred yards down the beach, and it was at about this distance that I saw the huge black form at the edge of the water. Knowing that it could only be a bear, I nosed the boat toward shore, letting it coast the 20 or so yards to shallow water.

In the rain, the bear couldn't see any better than I could, and the wind howled in my face so I felt sure that I could close the distance by at least half. And close it I did. The bear hadn't moved. The more I studied the bear, the larger he looked. The storm was, by now, getting really ugly, and I worried often whether my powder was dry. About the time that I settled into a shooting position, the bear finally moved.

But he didn't walk; he sort of slumped forward on his belly, like a walrus. It took a moment for what I was seeing to sink in, but when it did, I almost had a convulsion. It had to be the bear that the old timer told me about. I was exactly where he said that he'd seen it. And what was it that he said? … "He comes in on the storm!" Holy Fourth Dimension Batman! It was Old Three Legs!

By then things were getting a little strange for this bear hunter, but not about to be hocus-pocused out of a giant bear, I carefully capped my Knight rifle, trying to keep everything dry. I cocked the inline ignition. Shouldering the rifle, I aimed deliberately and increased the pressure on the trigger. My sight picture was foggy—I admit that—but the aim was dead on.

Old Three Legs didn't do anything at the report except turn like an inbound whale, and slump toward the safety of the thick rainforest half a football field away. Still unbelieving, it took me a moment to think about reloading my muzzleloader. All the while, Old Three Legs kept slumping toward the trees.

By the time that I was ready to shoot again, he was right at the edge of the forest. He stopped, and I fired. Again, no reaction. He just lunged and in a second was gone. Now I admit, I've

The author first considered the tales of ol' three legs the ramblings of a senile sailor. Then he crossed paths with the ancient bear for himself.

missed my fair share of shots over the years and I'll miss more in the future. But for the life of me I couldn't believe that I missed Old Three Legs twice.

Reloading before I headed between the sheets of rain to where he'd last been, I couldn't help thinking about what the old fellow said … what was it? "Old Three Legs can't be killed." Naw.

I looked for blood in the pouring rain—a futile effort at best—and found nothing. I was forced to call off the search when the lack of light made such work foolhardy at best and dangerous at worst.

By the time that I made it back to the truck, I was soaked, frozen and disgusted with myself. I couldn't do a thing until morning and since it was raining too hard to even think about putting up my tent, I cracked open a can of beans, ate them cold and went to sleep on the truck seat. I'm not sure how many times I woke up during the night, at least a dozen because I was cold and wet and at least another dozen because I couldn't get the sight picture out of my head. I had to have hit the bear with both shots. Ghost or not, nothing ever went far with two 310-grain slug holes through the boiler room.

In the morning the whole inlet was steaming as the sun began drying out the previous evening's dirty work. Within minutes I was back in my skiff and headed for the scene of the crime. Upon arrival, I looked hard for nearly two hours and found no sign. I was beginning to believe that the old weird guy and his Casper stories might be true. However, before I committed myself to an asylum, I made one last sweep farther along the shoreline.

And in the process, I found Old Three Legs. He'd circled back to the shoreline and died within yards of where I'd been searching. He was by far the largest-bodied bear I'd ever taken, and sure as shooting he only had three legs. One back leg was gone just below the knee.

It's hard to say what happened to his leg, but whatever it was, it happened a long time ago. He was battle scarred and old, and how he ever managed to survive so long with the number of cannibal bears around is beyond me. Maybe it was his massive size that kept him alive. He eventually ended up squaring an honest 7 feet, 2 inches and his skull measured a bit more than 20 inches. I never found evidence of the old pirate's claimed direct hit.

Never did see the old fellow or the Betsy Lee II again. I suppose stranger things have happened, but I still get the creeps about that old guy and that weird, stormy night. ∎

CHAPTER NINE:

THE HUNTED

Good tracking snow is heavenly. It falls upon the hunter's world gently, glazing the wild land, transforming it from a dark place of mystery—a place unfathomable—to a place exposed. One by one the snowflakes drop silky, until finally, naked, the wild land stands before the hunter, secrets revealed in completely complex beauty. Even the simplest hunter cannot help but gaze lustily upon such a land and, in so doing, become the greatest of seers. Good tracking snow is every hunter's crystal ball. The past, the present and the future become one … but this is not always a good thing.

"Um, Lance?" I tapped the back that had suddenly stopped in front of me.

"What?" Lance, my guide leaned back without turning, whispering the word.

"Correct me if I'm wrong," I said pointing ahead. "But aren't those our tracks?"

Lance didn't answer. He didn't need to. The chance of there being two other humans traipsing around the Tatshenshini River valley at the point where it joined the mighty Alsek River—literally the most remote place in British Columbia—was nil. The tracks were ours all right, from that morning and they were as

we'd left them, on top of an impressive set of pie-plate-sized grizzly tracks. Or they were until the impressive set of pie-plate-sized grizzly tracks we were following joined with our old trail. Then our tracks were sandwiched between the two sets of big bear tracks. Which, coincidentally, was exactly how I was beginning to feel … like a sandwich.

"The son-of-a-gun circled … he's circled us!" Lance finally spoke, again without taking his eyes off of the trail in front of us.

"Oh, that's wonderful news," I said trying to make light of the sick feeling in my gut. "Let me see if I have this straight. The bear we were following—the one that was ahead of us, is now behind us?"

Lance didn't say anything for a moment, but when he did, the words sent shivers up my spine.

"Not exactly," he said. "It means he's behind us and in front of us …"

As Lance and I stood quietly contemplating the tracks on top of our own, an errant snowflake drifted down to join the zillion others that lay on the ground. It hadn't snowed since first light when we'd pulled the boat onto the riverbank. At the time, tracking the grizzly had seemed like a pretty good idea. The magnificent set of tracks coursing the shoreline had been so obvious, so fresh in the new snow and so inviting that we couldn't help but follow them into the timber. Speaking for myself, I felt like a mouse who'd just heard the "sproing" of a trap.

At that point, with the willies pitter-pattering up and down my spine, I wasn't even considering the dignified option—a tactical withdrawal. I was thinking in far more visceral terms. Run away! Run away!

Only the thought of running face-first into a mouthful of big, sharp teeth stilled my winged feet. The bear was behind us somewhere.

"Nothing to do but follow," Lance said. He took a step forward. I took a step backward.

And so the next hour passed. Slowed by warning bells clanging in those deepest places of our brain where survival instincts live, we only covered 200 yards in that distressing hour. At the end of those 60 minutes of eternity, we found ourselves at a place where the big bear's fresher tracks left the trail, this time off the opposite side.

"What's he up to now?" Lance's icy eyes, buried beneath furrowed brow, searched the tracks for some clue.

My eyes searched for a suitable tree to climb. And still the snowflakes fell.

"Come on," Lance said taking up the new trail. Or he did until it became clear that the griz was circling back again!

"Oh shit," Lance said. "Look at that!"

The grizzly tracks had taken us up an almost imperceptible rise that we now realized was actually the backside of a rock bluff that jutted up from the forest floor. The front of the rock bluff dropped off nearly 100 feet to the forest floor, making it a perfect lookout. On the top of that perfect lookout was a perfect, fresh and very big grizzly bed—a very big grizzly bed without any snow in it. It didn't take Daniel Boone to unravel what that meant. It had been snowing since we first discovered that the bear was circling us; the bear had been lying in its bed watching us while we'd been discussing our options.

"Look at that!" Lance was pointing down through the treetops.

It was as easy as reading a cheap novel. There below us were our tracks coming from where we'd left the boat and there were our tracks coming back onto the trail at the point where we'd realized the bear had circled us.

"Lance?" I was getting a bad feeling about who was hunting whom. "When we were down there, we should have looked up here, right?"

Lance was looking at an alder tree a few yards away. The grizzly's tracks left the bed and went to the tree, or more correctly, what was left of it. It was torn to shreds. Bark and bits of tree guts lay everywhere, staining the fresh snow. Deep scars raked the tender white insides of the alder, ripping it from stem to stern. Ugly bite marks splintered the tortured softwood; the tree was dead.

"Think that's some kind of warning?" It didn't take much imagination to put one's self in the tree's place.

"Yeah," Lance answered.

"Well I don't scare that easy," I said, trying to be tough.

"Me either," Lance concurred.

"On the other hand, I'm getting kind of hungry," I said, taking a glance over my shoulder. "What say we head to the boat and have a bite … I mean something to eat, and come back later

to take up this track again?"

"Good idea," Lance said.

We never went back.

ENTER THE FRAY

If you spend time in the North American wilderness, you'll encounter a grizzly bear some day. Bang pots all you want, whistle when you walk and tie your food in a tree 10 miles from your campsite. It's inevitable. You will find a grizzly in your face one day.

And that's when you're not looking for one. When you're hunting for one of the great beasts, you purposely expose yourself to trouble. And, trust me, you will find it. Don't get me wrong, grizzly bears don't live behind every tree. At least they don't unless you've been scared by one in the past. Once that happens, they live behind every tree, under every rock and in every dream that you'll ever have.

In spite of this, if you're out hunting for one, chances are that you'll have to work to find and kill one of reasonable size. It took me 10 years of occasional grizzly hunting before I finally found the one that I wanted in a situation that allowed me to take a crack at him with my Knight muzzle-loader. I've considered that quest to be one long hunt, most of it relatively forgettable, but there certainly were moments that will forever remain clear in my mind. Moments of extreme excitement.

My quest for griz began when I was a relative greenhorn straight from the prairies, "looking to get me a bar in them thar hills." I'll never forget looking down and seeing my first grizzly track there in the mud like a misplaced manhole cover. It was longer than my size 12 boots and twice as wide!

The wall of trees on each side of the trail leaned in consuming me like an omen. Squirrel noises suddenly turned ominous and threatening and sort of carnivorous-sounding. My legs wobbled, and my heart pounded. I backed out of the forest along the trail. I backed all the way to camp and all the way to where the airplane was to pick me up. That fall I backed out of the opportunity to hunt grizzlies in the same area.

Granted, my first experience with grizzly bears

Who's tracking who? Hunting for a grizzly bear often leads one to wonder who the ultimate hunter is.

Chapter Nine: The Hunted

71

or, more correctly, with grizzly bear sign, wasn't exactly a close encounter. But you couldn't have told me that at the time. During the first few hunts after that experience, I can't say that I was keen on actually shooting at one. I guess if I could have found one across a deep canyon where I could shoot with impunity, I might have pulled the pin. But, for the most part, the situations that I found grizzlies in all felt too risky to chance a shot with my muzzleloader. Call it bear fever, if you'd like.

CLOSE ENCOUNTERS

One time, my hunting partner, Guy, and I waited for three days along a salmon stream before the bear appeared 600 yards away, making his way toward us; searching the banks of the river for salmon carcasses. The wind wasn't entirely wrong, but it certainly wasn't right. We had to get across the river fast to keep the wind from betraying us.

Quicker than it takes to tell it, we were stepping into the frigid river. It rose above our knees and then above our waists. Just as the icy water's grip began to suffocate me about the chest, I spotted the grizzly again.

He was much closer than before, now just 100 yards away staring at the two odd-looking logs sticking out of the water mid-stream. We froze figuratively and literally. We couldn't move without alerting the bear.

It seemed like an hour, but it really wasn't more than a minute or two before the bear took his eyes off of us and stepped into the water. Still holding my muzzleloader over my head, we continued toward shore. I held my possibles bag with my reloaders and powder in one hand and my muzzleloader in the other.

When the bear turned and started swimming closer, I started to tremble. There was some question in my mind whether I'd be able to shoot accurately, I was shaking so badly. But I needn't have worried. At 40 yards the grizzly looked up from his paddling and recognized us as human.

In a heartbeat he swapped ends and cut to the far bank. I could have killed him in the water, but that's illegal, so I waited for him to emerge on the far side. But when his feet hit ground all we could see was water spraying everywhere. There was no opportunity for a clean shot.

The author's cousin, Guy, killed this huge, blond grizzly when the bear made the hunters at just 30 yards.

The next day, from a new vantage, I'd just started glassing the mountainsides when I noticed a blond animal on a distant slope. Grizzly! A lighter-colored bear with dark legs.

After the production the day before, Guy and I were grim and determined to get this griz. In the spotting scope he looked like he might be big enough, and as we climbed the slope toward him we confirmed that he definitely was big enough. In the morning sun his blond coat stood out in shimmering contrast to the red leaves of the snowberry where he was standing. His powerful legs were black as coal.

Once we were within several hundred yards, we changed course to ease around a ridge in order to keep the wind right. Doing this meant losing sight of the bear for a time, but we were confident that he'd stay put grazing on the berries. When we poked our heads over the ridge he was just 30 yards away.

The range was easy, and the bear was unaware of our presence, so I turned to signal to Guy that I was going to shoot. When I looked back at the grizzly, I found myself looking right into his eyes! Some rotten, evil bit of wind swirled and warned the grizzly of our presence. We'd decided in advance that Guy would take over with his magnum rifle if there was any problem with the muzzleloader opportunity. I reached back and motioned frantically for Guy to stand and shoot the grizzly with his .338 Win. Mag.

Guy stood and picked up the griz in his scope all in one motion and commenced firing. The first shot was fatal, and so was the second. We knew it, but the griz didn't. It took a third to put the enraged beast down for good, a lesson in itself for all grizzly bear hunters. Make every shot count.

The Quest Continues

I never did complete my quest for a grizzly bear on that trip, but exactly one year and one month later I was back in the mountains. Outfitter Jack Goodwin accompanied me this time, but strictly for moral support and backup if necessary.

"There!" We both pointed at the same instant.

A moment before the gravel bar lay before us, barren, devoid of life. In fact, the entire mountain and valley lay desolate in the faded early morning light. Nothing moved. In a million years I wouldn't have believed that any life existed in that snow-covered wasteland.

I would have been wrong.

The pitch-black grizzly appeared suddenly, moving fast along the gravel bar. Even from our vantage point a quarter-mile away, the grizzly's dished-in face and characteristic hump were apparent, but it took a second look to see that he wasn't entirely black. Each time that he stepped, heavy and determined, a shimmer of silver rolled in a wave across his entire body.

Awesome.

Once we believed that the grizzly intended to continue on his way down the gravel bar, we moved. Grabbing the bare necessities for the short stalk, we scrambled down the slope to the valley bottom and raced on an instinctive intercept course that would, we hoped, put us within muzzleloader range.

Without the benefit of our vantage point, both the bear and open gravel bar were now out of our line of sight, obscured by head-high, nearly impenetrable tangled patches of buck brush. Branches whipped me in the face as we ran, stinging my cheek and causing me to duck, weave and block like a prize fighter. What a rush! My heart throttled as I juked around another tangle. Shivers of anticipation raced from my head to my toes and back again; the first warning signs of "the fever." My arms turned to rubber, and my legs wobbled. Suddenly, the scrub brush opened up, and we hit down on our knees gazing at the gravel bar.

Empty.

Truthfully, I wasn't prepared to shoot. With a high-power rifle maybe, but not with a muzzleloader. If that black silvertip grizzly had been there in front of us or if I would have had to watch him work along the gravel bar toward us, I believe that I would have fallen apart; resolve replaced by quivering insecurity.

Early that morning, just before first light, it had snowed; not for long, but long enough to cover the entire valley in a glistening skiff. Anything moving since dawn left obvious sign of passage. Jack and I looked for this sign as we eased along the gravel bar toward where we'd last seen the bear.

We hit the tracks close to where we expected to find them, and one look was enough to confirm that the bear had changed his mind about walking in the open shortly after we took up the stalk. Instead, he'd turned and cut back into the 50-acre, river-bottom patch of buck brush that he'd originally crawled out of. I would have quit tracking the grizzly right there at the edge of the buck brush, but Jack seemed determined to follow the tracks into the grizzly bear's stomach.

A couple hundred feet into the tangled brushy patch, three things became apparent. The first was that the patch was more open than I'd imagined. We could see nearly 50 yards in some spots. The second was that the ground was covered in low soapberry bushes—a grizzly bear fall favorite. The third was the fact that there was a second grizzly bear somewhere in the 50-acre patch with us. … A bigger grizzly.

Jack bent over and examined the new tracks crossing those that we were following. There was no doubt about it; made that morning and a full inch wider across the front pad! For the first time since we started in on the track, Jack and I agreed on something.

Retreat!

We did, cutting through the brush toward the relative safety of the open gravel bar. As you might expect, I stayed close to Jack on the way out, so close that when he stopped just before stepping out onto the gravel bar, I bumped into him. He didn't even notice. At his feet was a third set of tracks. I reached down and spread my hand apart. The distance between the end of my thumb and the end of my middle finger is 9 inches exactly. It didn't take a rocket scientist to see that whatever made the track had a front pad nearly 1 inch wider than my spread hand.

"Sasquatch?" I asked hopefully.

"Brown bear probably," Jack whispered.

Jack's territory, located in the most remote northwest corner of British Columbia is home to the highest concentration of grizzly bears in North America and the dividing line where the record book differentiates grizzlies and coastal (Alaska) brown bears. Regardless of size, any bear killed in Jack's territory is considered by every record-keeping organization, to be a grizzly.

NEVER SAY DIE?

"Can we go home now, Jack?" My muzzle-loader felt puny and inadequate. So did I.

"No," Jack said, setting out for our original vantage point. "We're going to sit up there until we see one of these grizzlies."

"I was worried you might say that," I replied keeping a sharp eye peeled over my shoulder as we walked. "Did I tell you that I'm allergic to grizzly bear slobber?"

For 30 minutes after we reached the lookout, Jack never moved except to shift his Leupold spotting scope this way or that. His eye never left the scope as he tried to pick up some small bit of fur in the berry patch.

"Got him!" he whispered.

I whipped my spotting scope around to the coordinates that Jack described.

"He stood up down there," Jack said, still glued to the spotting scope as he spoke. "He was checking the wind."

"Same bear?" I asked.

"No. Different." Jack was about to say some-

thing more when he stopped. "There!"

What a beauty! The grizzly's black face stood out in high relief from its powerful sloping silver-blond shoulders. Then as quickly as it appeared, the bear dropped to all fours and disappeared.

Half an hour later the beautiful two-tone grizzly appeared again. This time it was headed out of the berry patch and up the mountainside. For a minute the bear would be in sight and then for five more we'd lose it. As the ground cover thickened, the time periods without us seeing the bear lengthened. Eventually the grizzly simply vanished.

"He's bedded," Jack said with finality.

"So what now?" I asked, relieved in one way and disappointed in another. "Did we lose him?"

"No," Jack said, training his spotting scope into the berry patch once again. "He'll come down again to feed this evening. Maybe we'll see the other two while we wait."

For five hours, we waited.

Just into the sixth hour, the dirty yellow-looking boulder that I'd been watching up on the mountainside started walking down toward the berry patch.

"Grizzly!" I exclaimed.

We didn't need to speak, we knew what we had to do. For the second time that day, Jack and I grabbed our gear and raced headlong through the buck brush. The first time I'd run with wild abandon, but not this time. As we ran, I forced myself to methodically repeat the pre-ignition checklist.

Safety one, safety two, cocked, cap on. Safety one, safety two, cocked, cap on.

The checklist ran through my mind like a soothing mantra, keeping my nerves calm and my mind off of the imminent showdown.

We skirted the berry patch, working instead along the far edge where it met the mountainside. Jack was hoping to catch the grizzly before it fed too far into the berry patch.

"Jack!" I reached ahead to grab him, but he was already stopped, eyes fixed on the blond grizzly's head and shoulders showing above the buck brush 100 yards away.

"He heard us," Jack whispered urgently back over his shoulder. "Get ready!"

Without taking my eyes off of the grizzly, I stepped forward and around Jack. The bear

Partnering with veteran big game guide, Jack Goodwin, the author finally killed his first grizzly after many fruitless attempts. The bear fell just 14 steps from the author.

dropped from sight, back to all fours. There was nothing we could do but wait breathlessly for the events to unfold.

We didn't have to wait long.

The grizzly appeared 60 yards away, walking stiff-legged toward us.

With a high-powered rifle, the hunt would have been over right then, but armed as I was with a muzzleloader, the grizzly offered me no certain killing shot.

At 40 yards I heard the safety on Jack's .30-06 click off.

The big grizzly continued toward us. Huge and menacing. The distance closed ... 30 yards ... 20 yards ...

I don't remember the grizzly doing it, but at some point he angled slightly to one side, aiming to pass just by us. I do, however, remember his black fearsome eyes. I will always remember his eyes. They never left mine as he padded silently toward me.

Finally the grizzly stopped. He was still quartering toward me; my muzzleloader had long since come to shoulder, safety off.

I didn't breathe.

Without taking his eyes off of mine, the grizzly turned broadside. For a split-second his rib cage filled my scope, and in that second I fired.

I vaguely remember the huge beast dropping in his tracks. And I vaguely remember my hands shaking so badly I had to get Jack to hold my muzzleloader steady while I poured another load of powder down the barrel. Those things are vague, but I distinctly remember Jack's words as I reloaded.

"He's up!"

Sweet Mother of Jesus!

In a slow lifetime I finished loading and brought the rifle to my shoulder, firing as I did at the huge form moving in the buck brush in front of me.

Hit hard the first time, the grizzly was mobile but disoriented. The second bullet broke him down again. And once again I reloaded. And once again I distinctly remember Jack's warning.

"He's up!"

No! Not again!

It took another slow lifetime to reload and bring the muzzleloader on target. But this time at the booming report, the grizzly went down for good.

My body shook violently. Jack's eyes never left the dead grizzly as he pulled out the makings and deliberately rolled a cigarette. Then he put it in the side of his mouth and stepped off 14 short paces to the spot where the grizzly had been standing when I first fired.

"I want my mommy," I said. Jack just smiled. ∎

CHAPTER TEN:
THE RING OF FIRE

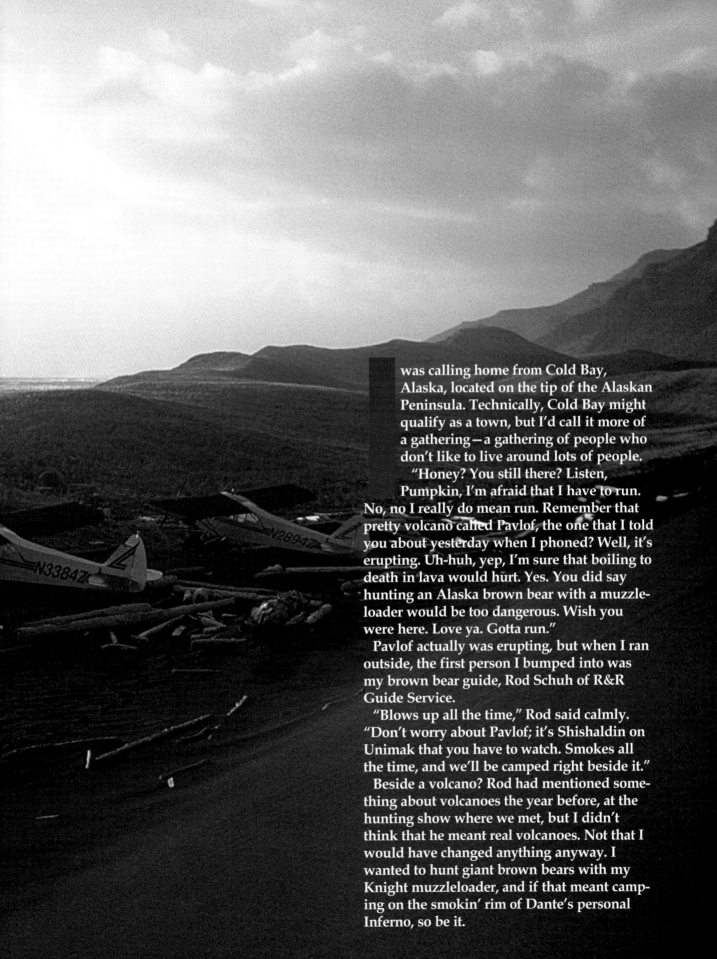

was calling home from Cold Bay, Alaska, located on the tip of the Alaskan Peninsula. Technically, Cold Bay might qualify as a town, but I'd call it more of a gathering—a gathering of people who don't like to live around lots of people.

"Honey? You still there? Listen, Pumpkin, I'm afraid that I have to run. No, no I really do mean run. Remember that pretty volcano called Pavlof, the one that I told you about yesterday when I phoned? Well, it's erupting. Uh-huh, yep, I'm sure that boiling to death in lava would hurt. Yes. You did say hunting an Alaska brown bear with a muzzle-loader would be too dangerous. Wish you were here. Love ya. Gotta run."

Pavlof actually was erupting, but when I ran outside, the first person I bumped into was my brown bear guide, Rod Schuh of R&R Guide Service.

"Blows up all the time," Rod said calmly. "Don't worry about Pavlof; it's Shishaldin on Unimak that you have to watch. Smokes all the time, and we'll be camped right beside it."

Beside a volcano? Rod had mentioned some-thing about volcanoes the year before, at the hunting show where we met, but I didn't think that he meant real volcanoes. Not that I would have changed anything anyway. I wanted to hunt giant brown bears with my Knight muzzleloader, and if that meant camp-ing on the smokin' rim of Dante's personal Inferno, so be it.

Rod and his partner, Rob Jones, run one of only two outfits authorized to conduct guided brown bear hunts on Unimak Island, a small 25-mile by 50-mile volcanic island located just off the tip of the Alaskan Peninsula. Unimak sits squarely on what's referred to as the Ring of Fire; a circle of active volcanoes that bisects the Pacific Ocean. It's also located within the boundaries of the Izembeck National Wildlife Refuge. Unimak deserves more recognition than it gets. It arguably harbors the densest population of brown bears in Alaska—a fact that I was lucky enough to confirm firsthand during the fall of 1996.

I was one of 15 hunters to be drawn for the annual limited-entry brown bear hunt. Every year, eight hunters are drawn for the fall hunt and seven for the spring hunt. Mostly, though, I was lucky enough to hunt on Unimak because I happened to hook up with the boys from R&R. If I wouldn't have met them, I never would have even applied for the hunt in the first place. Rod and Rob walked me through the simple process of applying for and drawing a permit.

I remember liking Rod and Rob the first time I

Wander around an Alaskan salmon stream long enough in the fall and you'll land an Alaska brown bear in your lap.

stopped by their booth at the show. Their brochure claimed, "Where hunting and adventure are one and the same." After hunting with them, I can honestly say amen to that.

My adventure started during the middle of October at the Reeves Aleutian Airline gate in Anchorage. When the Reeves Aleutian jet landed in Cold Bay, I was met by Rod, Rob and Beaufort Force 8 winds that would keep us from flying to Unimak for two days. Good thing too, I got to see Pavlof erupt, which is an adventure in itself. The brown bear part of the adventure started during the flight to Unimak in one of R&R's two customized Super Cubs. That's when I saw my first real, live Alaska brown bear.

It stood up on its hind legs as we passed high overhead and it looked huge. Rod, piloting the Super Cub, told me it wasn't much over 8 feet—way too small to bother hunting even though I was shooting a muzzleloader. Before

Rod touched down on the black silica sand beach, I'd counted three more bears.

"There isn't a single tree! There's hardly any alder brush either!" I said in amazement, as we turned in the sand anchors that would hold the airplane in place while we hunted. "You can see for miles!"

"Exactly," Rod confirmed. "That's one of the reasons that it's such a great place to hunt."

"What's the other reason?" I asked.

Rod nodded his head toward the ocean. "Check out the beach," he said.

I did and, quite frankly, I got a little scared. There were bear tracks everywhere. Big ones, little ones, old ones and new ones. Some were gigantic. Obviously, Unimak was a place where you wanted to spend a lot of time looking over your shoulder.

"The bears roam the beaches searching for washed up whale carcasses," Rod explained to me later. "We're not staying by the beach, though, we're going to backpack a few miles inland, set up camp and glass the grass flats and the salmon streams."

ALL-OUT ADVENTURE

And that's exactly what we did for the next 15 days. From the spot where we eventually set up camp and on the days that we were able to glass, we saw at least five brown bears every day. Most days we saw nine to 10 bears, and there were three days when we counted 13 different ones. In short, there were bears everywhere—including right in our camp two nights in a row!

This is Rod's version of what happened those two nights.

"WOOOOFFF!"

"Hey Jim? Did you hear that?" he whispered.

"WOOOOOOOOOOOFFFFFF!!!!"

"Dang!" Rod cursed and grabbed his rifle and headlamp.

"SNORT!"

"Don't move, he's right beside the tent," he warned.

"WOOOFFF!"

"HEY GET OUTTA HERE!!!" Rod yelled and slapped the tent wall.

__Unimak Island is a small, volcanic island off the tip of the Alaska Peninsula.__

Ultimate Big Game Adventures

If you're expecting wild weather and a wild, untamed land, Unimak, the author discovered, offers all of that and then some. His host for the hunt, R&R Adventures, describes its hunts as "where hunting and adventure are one and the same."

Silence.

"Jim, he's gone. Jim?" Rod jabbed me with his finger.

"Huh?" I sat up and rubbed my eyes. "What's up?"

"There was a bear right outside the tent!"

"Huh? What was that about the right way to make cement?"

I slept through both adventures. As I should have. I couldn't hear a thing. Rod snores, so every night I shoved big balls of wet toilet paper into my ears. I also pulled the earflaps on my hat down and tied my long underwear around the whole affair. I looked like I had a toothache, but I slept like a baby.

That was a bear adventure, but there were weather adventures as well. Like the night and day when the "Willy Wahs" blasted us. Rob and R&R video cameraman, John, joined Rod and I halfway through my hunt, both to re-supply us and to get some video footage. We were all stuffed into the small tent, visiting late one evening, when Rob cocked his head.

"Hang on to your hats," he said, crouching even lower in the cramped tents. "Beware the Willy Wah!"

A roaring sound from somewhere above us on the nearby volcano grew louder and closer and then ... WHAM! The tent nearly turned inside out … with us in it!

A Willy Wah, I very quickly learned, is a meteorological mutation, an airborne aberration, a 100-yard-wide landslide of cold air that comes

roaring down from a mountain top at speeds of up to 100 miles an hour! It's the wildest thing to hear and is even wilder to see.

All that night I cowered in my sleeping bag listening to Willy Wahs roaring down the side of Isanotski, the closest snow-capped volcano. Most missed us, thank God, but when they hit broadside, even though our tent was hunkered down deep in an alder patch, it was like getting hit by a tent-sized sledgehammer. The instant change in pressure literally took your breath away.

At least we could hunt in the Willy Wahs. They came and went, flattening everything in their way for a few minutes as they beat a path to the ocean. Not so when we were hit, for three days straight, by Beaufort Force 11 winds. To put that into perspective, we're talking sustained winds of 70 miles an hour and 30- to 40-foot waves on an ocean that turns into a white frothing maelstrom! I'd say that the wind drift on my muzzleloader bullet would have been nearly four feet or so at 100 yards.

Why the unusual weather on Unimak Island? Well, it's located smack in the middle of nowhere, sandwiched between the bitter cold Bering Sea and the gigantic Pacific Ocean. There's nothing to keep a breeze from growing into a hurricane. In other words, when someone sneezes in Tokyo and you're standing on Unimak, those little "made in Japan" germs hit you in the face like the Orient Express.

Experiencing the weather on Unimak was an adventure, to say the least, but muzzleloading

for the giant Alaska brown bears that stomp all over the island goes beyond adventure. We stalked and turned down numerous bears that would have squared close to 9 feet—respectable brown bears most places, but not on Unimak Island. On Unimak you have every right to expect a chance at a bear that will square more than 9 feet and, if you're lucky, over the magic 10-foot barrier. Rod and Rob have taken bears on the island that square more than 10½ feet.

On one stalk, Rod and I sneaked to within 46 yards of a sleeping 9-foot-plus boar. We then hunkered down in a patch of grass and waited for three hours for the respectable bear to stand up so that I would have a clear shot. Unfortunately for us, when he did finally stand up, he went out like a rocket and disappeared over the hill without giving me a chance to shoot.

We were disappointed for sure, but things could have turned out worse, we learned. John was taping us the whole time from a nearby hill. He told us that while we were lying there waiting for the first bear to get up, another bear had walked up to within 30 yards of us! Not only that, a pure white wolf walked up to us on the other side at the same time. The wolf came within 100 yards. We hadn't seen either the wolf or the other bear, but we couldn't deny

Usually you don't have to look hard to find a brown bear on Unimak, since it harbors one of the highest bear densities in Alaska.

that it happened because John captured the near tragedy on tape!

ULTIMATE SHOWDOWN

Unfortunately, as every adventure must, my adventure on Unimak Island was drawing to a close, and it was getting to be time to shoot a bear. We knew where one big boar's favorite fishing hole was, so we set up on a high vantage and waited for him to step out from whatever small patch of alder he was bedded in.

During the middle of the afternoon the first day we hunted him, he appeared right by his fishing hole where we expected him. Rob and John stayed high on the nearest hill to videotape the hunt, while Rod and I went after the fishing bruin.

Adventure is addictive. Once you get hooked, you need bigger adventures and more of them to keep your desire's need satisfied. That said, I can honestly say that stalking up on that big brown bear on Unimak Island was the ultimate to that point in my hunting adventures. At one point, we were only 30 yards from him, but I

Testament to their toughness, this 9 ½-foot boar took three well-placed shots before it finally fell.

couldn't get a clear shot. He towered over us, giving me a real appreciation for the word "insignificant."

When the bear finally turned and offered a shot, I fired. (I later found that first perfectly mushroomed Barnes X bullet lodged in the bear's heart.) He heaved into the alders, and I reloaded. The instant that I finished ramming the big bullet down the barrel, as if on cue, he came back out of the alders to see what insignificant thing was bothering him. Boom! That second bullet fully penetrated the huge animal's lungs and lodged under the skin on the far side. The bear spun back into the alders again.

Nearly five minutes after my first bullet lodged in the animal's heart, and 400 yards from where he originally stood, I squeezed the trigger again, finishing the 9½-foot boar.

As we walked up to that bear, there was no doubt that, just as their brochure had promised, Rod and Rob had taken me to a place where hunting and adventure were one and the same. ∎

Chapter Ten: The Ring Of Fire

CHAPTER ELEVEN:
TOE-TO-TOE

Warm bed, cold deer hunt? Warm bed, cold deer hunt? My alarm had just gone off, and I couldn't decide. It seemed pointless to repeat the futility of the day before: Crawl out of my nice, warm bed, dress in a half-dozen layers of thermal clothing, step into the pre-dawn deep freeze, drive bleary-eyed to my hunting area and then crunch uselessly through the 6 inches of ice-crusted snow all day. Warm bed.

Two hours later, I remained tucked beneath the covers.

But then the guilt became too much. It was, after all, the last week of the season. I reminded myself that I had been raised a devout whitetail hunter, and no one ever shot a big buck from his nice, warm bed. So with the guilt of starting my hunting day two hours later than I should have, and the knowledge that my greatest hope for success rested with Lady Luck, I dressed and headed out.

The sun high above the eastern horizon by the time that I stepped from my truck served constant reminder to my slacking dedication. And it did little to warm my spirits. The second day of the last week of the 1990 Saskatchewan whitetail season dawned minus 20, clear and dead calm. Dreadful weather for a deer hunter on foot.

Because it was so late, I decided that rather than take the circuitous approach as I had the day before, it would do no harm to take the most direct route. Positive that so late in the morning any whitetails would be long into the cover, I shouldered my pack and the guilt for sleeping in and started climbing the river breaks to the sand hills perched on the edge of the Saskatchewan river valley.

The area on top where I had permission to hunt is superb whitetail country. On the route that I chose to take to the top, I would crest the hill at a spot where I would be looking across nearly 400 yards of rolling pasture. As an afterthought, just before I topped the rise, I waited for several minutes to catch my breath. It is one of those silly things you learn to do when you hunt trophy whitetails—especially when you know that there isn't a big buck within 1,000 miles.

WHEN YOU LEAST EXPECT IT...

As my breathing slowed and the rushing sound in my ears cleared, I suddenly heard what sounded like cattle crunching around in the ice-covered snow on the flats just out of my sight beyond the ridge. But I knew that there were no cattle in the pasture.

It is rare to have white-tailed deer dead to rights, but that is exactly what I had stumbled into. Checking to ensure that I had a cap on the nipple of my Knight muzzleloader and the safety on, I removed my felt packs and proceeded, in stocking feet, the last few steps to where I would be able to see out into the pasture. Every agonizing step, even in stocking feet, sounded like thunder to me, but the hill shielded the sound from the deer.

The first whitetail that I saw was a small buck. There, another small buck. A third and fourth buck; one small, the other respectable, but still young—not yet in his prime and not yet of interest to me. The fifth buck to appear was a spike hot on the heels of a young doe. My heart hammered harder as I scanned for the big buck that I knew must be near. For several minutes I gawked as the bucks made the poor doe's life a loving hell. A sixth young buck appeared from behind a knoll in the field.

Then, as if on cue, the whole bunch seemed to notice that the sun had turned the landscape into a frosted white Christmas card wonderland. Not the best camouflage for a herd of deer. They turned from the pasture and began to make their way to the distant safety of the poplars.

Watching them cross the pasture, I almost jumped out of my long underwear. There on the edge of the poplars stood the buck that I knew must be near to so much whitetail rutting action. All I could see was his chin and head and, of course, his rack sticking out like a sore thumb against the white hoar frost. Cool as a cucumber I yanked my binoculars into place and exhaled warm air onto the lenses. Fogged beyond hope, I dropped them and lifted my Leupold scope just in time to see that his rack extended to the tip of his nose. I hadn't been quick enough to count points.

Then he was gone.

PLAN A

Struggling to control my ragged breathing and pounding heart, I formulated a plan. Familiar with the turf, I knew that the bush that the herd of deer entered was shaped like a Y. Because it was so late in the morning, I concluded that they would likely move along the stem and then bed in one of the forks. If I ran along below the ridge, I figured, I could get into position along the closest fork before they arrived. If they dawdled at all messing around with the doe, I'd make it for sure. And if the doe came my way, the buck surely would.

Twenty minutes later, I was in place and could see across the fork. Three hours and 20 minutes later, I was still in place and cold. It was apparent that the deer had chosen the far fork. Then I did what I should not have done.

Logic and all of the hunting experts who write for deer hunting magazines would have said wave the white flag for the morning. Return in the evening or the next morning they would have advised. Best to leave him alone and not risk spooking him out of the country. Yet, I chose to go after him in the bush with the dead calm and crunching snow stacking the odds steeply against me.

PLAN B

For the second time in the day I removed my felt packs, only this time I wore only the felt inner booties. It was a trick that I had learned from my hunting partner in Alberta, Jim Krissa. Many times I have doubted my own ability to hunt whitetails, but never have I doubted Jim's.

He told me once that you can hunt for several hours in below-zero weather wearing only your felts. They act as a convenient and surprisingly quiet pair of moccasins in a pinch like the one that I was in.

I vowed that I could only continue the hopeless hunt on two conditions. First, I had to walk on my tip-toes. Second, I would walk in staccato bursts with many stops. By moving on my toes, I intended to sound like a buck in search of does.

I decided not to walk slowly either. I would stop, look and listen before taking several quick steps forward and stopping again. Sometimes the stops were long, sometimes short, always they were erratic. I sounded like a deer.

I covered several hundred yards through the sand-hill and poplar mix without seeing a deer, and my legs were beginning to quake from the effort. Near the end of the far fork in the Y-shaped bush, I climbed a small knoll that overlooked a 100-yard-long rose bush-choked basin on one side and the poplar bush on the other side.

The buck was already on the move through the waist-high rose bushes by the time that I looked into the basin. He was not in a panic run, but instead trotted stiff-legged at an angle that would bring him closer to me and higher on the side of the basin.

I flicked the safety off and remember thinking that if ever there was a time to make a shot count this was it. Yet I didn't know how much to lead a trotting buck at 80 yards. As I was about to squeeze the shot, it occurred to me the buck was not attempting to get away but was instead trying to see what I was.

I held my fire, and an instant later the buck cleared the rose bushes and stopped on the side hill. To this day, I can picture him standing broadside looking at me. Every hair stood in fine focus in the bright sunlight. Every breath flared in a cloud, and every muscle rippled. To this day, I think that he believed that I was another buck.

The sight picture was perfect. At the booming report, the buck turned and fled up and over the far side of the basin. His tail was down, and I remember hearing his antlers striking the frozen poplar branches on the far side out of my sight. Then nothing. It was for all the world as if the

Sometimes, to kill a whitetail, you have to improvise. Despite crunchy snow, the author still-hunted his way to this trophy buck.

sequence of events had never happened.

I looked down into the basin to where the buck had appeared and then I knew why he had been so aggressive. The doe lay in the rose bushes. We watched each other for several minutes. It seemed as though the sound of the shot startled her, but not enough to dispel her belief that there was another buck just over the rise. She must have been disappointed when I stepped into full view.

I found him 50 yards over the hill.

I stopped several yards away and reflected on the morning, the odd way that it began and ended. I congratulated myself on taking the old buck and thanked Mother Nature. I walked over and raised his head. ■

Chapter Twelve:

The Fire In His Eye

hen you penetrate a trophy whitetail's perimeter defenses; when you get close enough to hear him breathe, to see the flame explode in his eyes; when the strongest sense, the sixth, suddenly rams electricity through every steel fiber in his body, then you can say that you have taken a trophy whitetail ... nature's ultimate survivor.

Perfect. Everything. The wind touched my face, gently, while the noon sun changed the snow to quiet, wet cotton. The shadows in the fresh track 20 feet to my left were easy to see, though the track itself was already melted and looked days old. I had been on the track for an hour, 200 yards.

One step, look for a minute.

One step, look for two.

Even in the thick bush, the trail turned to almost impenetrable. Now finger-sized, head-high saplings filled the few gaps between the poplars. One step, look for a minute. Another step, look for two. No great skill, just grinding discipline.

Now I know what old Pete meant. "Believe ... always believe," he said. "At the end of every deer track there is a deer."

Your mind tends to wander when you are on a track. Mine kept floating back over the last six weeks. Six weeks of waiting for one chance at an old white-tailed buck. Six weeks of disappointment. Two steps, look for half-a-minute. My pessimistic side felt assured that this day would end as another lesson in futility. Might as well get it over with and push through the thick stuff. Three steps, scan ahead for a few seconds. Why bother?

Believe! Get control. Discipline. I tried to summon old Pete's promise. One step, look for one minute.

But pessimism lurked. One minute of looking 40 feet for something that might be standing 41 feet away. At that distance, I would hear him breathing before I saw him. Might as well crash right through. At least then I would see a tail to confirm that I was on the right track.

No! Discipline. Concentrate. I clinged to fleeting hope. One step, look for two minutes.

Another step, another minute.

This time should have been easier than all the others. I knew that the buck was the type of old warrior whitetail that I loved to pursue. Two hunters had seen him go into the bush and they said that he was all antlers.

THE SIXTH SENSE

One step, look for two minutes. This had to be the opportunity for which I'd sacrificed so much time and effort. Concentrate.

One step, no! Something. Was it movement? A leaf in the breeze? Don't move ... wait. Listen. Scrutinize.

It must have been that fine white line, canted slightly in the vertical maze. A weed? Thirty-five feet away, no more, maybe less. Wait ... wait. Another minute, that makes five. The white line wavered in the wind, a weed. No! It twitched.

The white line suddenly leapt into focus. Fine white hairs along the edge of ... a tail! Was it the buck? One minute ... another.

Movement! Ten feet closer and far to one side. The line of a back, neck and head. Suddenly the complete outline of an animal, a doe, standing there the whole time. Now the tail of the other deer moved and disappeared from the tiny space in the saplings. There it is filling another. Shoot now? At what? Maybe it's another doe? Wait. What if it moves out of view? Shoot now? No! Discipline. Wait.

"Gone," pessimism screamed inside of me. "Move quickly to see better." No! Discipline. Has to be there. Look low. Must have turned to the doe. Head must be down. Look low. There! A tine! God! At least 12 inches long, shoot! No. At what?

There! Above the tine, brown hair. Must be the back. Slowly, slowly, bring the rifle up. Look for the brown patch. Nothing. Too close! The scope is set too high. Shoot! No! Where's the patch?! Shoot anyway. No!

Lower the rifle and look over the scope. Shoot! No! Look ... there!

Now the scope. Yes, see it! Shoot! No! Squeeze.

The old buck carried a crown of 10 absolutely even, long points and two small stickers at the burr. And I had taken him hunting like a wolf and heeding the wisdom of old Pete, close enough to see the fire in his eye. ■

90

At the end of every track, there is a deer. With that simple knowledge and focused discipline, the author found this Saskatchewan buck.

Chapter Twelve: The Fire In His Eye

CHAPTER THIRTEEN:

'BIG' KODIAK DEER HUNT

Rocky Morgan, now there's a name that smacks of all things Alaskan. It's a big name (317 pounds big), a hard name (bounces in the meanest bar in Seward, Alaska during the off season) and a wild and tough name (guides on Kodiak Island and fights giant bears for fun). Huh? That's right, fights giant bears for fun. I remember the first time that I heard the name Rocky Morgan. …

"In this corner, weighing in at 800 pounds is Caesar the giant Alaska brown bear, and in this corner, at 210 is Caesar's lunch!"

The crowd roared its approval. The bell rang, and, exactly four seconds later, Caesar's lunch was lying on the ground screaming uncle. The hapless contender had paid $40 for the chance to wrestle Caesar and win the $1,000 prize offered to anyone who could pin the wrestling bruin. Needless to say, Caesar, sans leather and chain muzzle strap and replete with all of his teeth and claws, had never lost a match.

After they removed the 210 pounds of slob-bered up pretzel, the announcer began looking for another taker. "Come on, isn't there a real man in the bunch of youse!" Go figure, but the crowd, ostensibly there to attend the 1995, Grand Rapids, Michigan Sports Show fell into dead silence; no one dared wiggle.

Then from some dark recess at the back of the crowd a big voice boomed, "I'll take a piece of that bar'!" And a mountain moved; the crowd parted like the Sea of Galilee, and Rocky Morgan entered the ring.

The bell rang, and the war waged. Rocky grabbed the huge beast by the front leg and flipped it like an 800-pound pancake. Caesar retaliated with a mighty right and then a left to Rocky's center of gravity. Rocky dropped to a three-point stance and then lunged, bowling the big bear over for the second time in the match. One! Two! The crowd drowned out the referee. No three count! The crowd went crazy! WHAM! Caesar landed a hay-maker to Rocky's head! Big mistake. Rocky got angry. And the fight turned

ugly. Jabs! Counters! Hooks! A frightening combination. Ouch! Youch! Gasp! Caesar's weight advantage came into play.

Anyone who says that a human head (even an XXL human head) won't fit inside of an 800-pound brown bear's mouth, is wrong. Rocky got to meet Caesar's tonsils. Caesar flipped Rocky around by the head for what seemed like a full minute before spitting him out. Pi-too-ee!

The crowd was aghast! Even the paramedics on site were stunned into inaction! Was Rocky dead? Caesar stood, chest heaving, wondering and perhaps hoping the same thing.

Then, like the first shudder of an approaching earthquake, the mass of Alaskan bigness moved. Rocky was alive! Still no one in the crowd breathed as Rocky, bleeding from what was left of his face rose to his feet.

The crowd expected the words "I give up" but what they got were the words "Is that the best ya got?"

The last 27 seconds of the match will go down in bear wrestling history. When the bell rang, ending the fight, Rocky and Caesar were toe to toenail, duking it out. By all accounts, they both appeared to be smiling.

Which all brings us around to the phone call I received. On the other end was my good friend Bill Farley.

"Hey Jim, want to go hunting on Kodiak for Sitka blacktails?" Bill said, asking the question that I'd hoped to hear for years.

"Just give me the times and dates and I'll book my flights!" I said. I couldn't wait to hang up, but I asked one more question. "By the way, who's the outfitter?"

"Some guy named Rocky Morgan," Bill replied.

"Gulp." I nearly dropped the phone. "Rocky Morgan? Thee Rocky Morgan?" I asked.

"Must be," Bill said. "How many Rocky Morgan's can there be?"

Big Adventure

"Good to meet you Mr. Morgan, Sir," I said, reaching to shake the ham quarter that Rocky held out to me. "Hey you must have had a great plastic surgeon! Your face looks better."

"My face?" Rocky asked.

"Grand Rapids! What a fight!" I said, still in disbelief that I was actually shaking the ham of Rocky Morgan. "Everyone thought you were dead!"

"Oh that," Rocky said, hardy-har-haring as he recalled the event. "Figured I'd finish the fight and sew myself up, do it all the time, but when I saw my face in a mirror, I let them take me to the hospital."

Here I have to tell you that even though I hadn't actually hunted Sitka deer yet, I'd already had a great hunt. Not only because Rocky Morgan was bigger than life but because all of Alaska is bigger than life! We, the other members of the hunting party and I, had flown from Seattle to Anchorage and from there to Kodiak Island; it was like flying back in time; fog shrouded the yellow hillsides. Everything looked damp and ancient. No, everything was damp and ancient! Everything was so big!

We overnighted in Kodiak and the next day climbed into the Seahawk Air Beaver for the final stage of the journey. We ducked and wove our way through the clouds and fog banks, dipped under the radar and roared down the fiord to the secluded bay where Rocky holds court. Breathtaking! Rafts of every kind of weird, humpty-billed duck known to science bobbed as our wake slapped the alder-gagged shoreline. Yes, it had already been a great hunt.

Garnished with all the comforts of home, Rocky's working camp left nothing to be desired.

The food was great, guides excellent and stories … well, they were big (especially Rocky's)! Each morning we'd awaken to the smell of bacon and eggs, eat and wait for Rocky to assign us guides; then off we'd go in small aluminum boats destined for this or that cove or drainage. Not surprisingly, the hunt was fairly physical. We'd ditch the boat and climb through the tangled alders for the first hour or so until we broke through to the grassy alpine. Then we'd start hunting.

The first evening out, my guide, Tim Roads, didn't waste any time locating a good buck, it took about 20 seconds once we cleared alder. Following Rocky's instructions to take the first good buck we saw, I raised my muzzleloader and touched the trigger. The Knight boomed, and the big slug found the mark. The heavy-antlered, 100-or-so-pound, 3-by-3 buck didn't take 10 steps before dropping to the Kodiak alpine.

All the way up through the alders we'd come across sign left by Kodiak Island brown bears, the largest bears in the world; ursine "private property" signs as it were. Needless to say, the photo session was short and the skinning and quartering session, shorter. We were back at the lodge long before dark, a good place to be in light of everyone else's reports.

"Ten bucks, five bears," one hunter reported.

"We saw 11 bucks and three bears," another offered.

"Only saw four bucks and two bears," Bill explained. "But that's because we were too busy skinning my two bucks!"

Bill was tagged out with two beautiful first-day 4-by-5 Sitka deer.

In fact, during the ensuing days, all the hunters in our group tagged good bucks, all with the double throat patches that Sitka deer are famous for. I took another on the second day, a great buck that only missed becoming the Longhunter Society world record by a quarter of an inch. Blaine Morgan, Rocky's brother, led me out into the zero visibility, dripping fog, up a bear trail to a ridge that he insisted would produce a good buck.

"A buck is going to walk right by us," Blaine explained to his skeptical client who wondered why we were groping around in dangerous bear territory for Sitka deer instead of sitting by the

The author's first Kodiak buck proved that the Sitka might be the most handsome deer of all.

warm, dry fire. "We don't need to see more than 100 yards on this ridge, all we need to do is wait."

As far as I was concerned, Blaine was wrong on at least one count, we needed to see more than 100 yards to have any chance of avoiding a hungry Kodiak brown bear. As it turned out, the buck showed before the bear, and we were back in camp in time to dry out before dinner.

The largest buck taken by our group, was a monster Boone and Crockett record book 5-by-5, taken by West Virginian, Tim Moore. And, more importantly, when it was all said and done, none of us had any close calls with bears, … at least nothing to rival Rocky Morgan's. ∎

CHAPTER FOURTEEN:

THE BADDEST BLACKTAIL

Discussions about which deer species is the most difficult to hunt, invariably end nowhere; mostly because the majority of us are either whitetail hunters or mule deer hunters and are incapable of being objective.

But having hunted them all, most of them many times, I have an opinion … take it for what it's worth. Hunting a trophy Columbia black-tailed deer is almost always a lesson in humility—one that I have learned all too well, thank you very much. It took this whitetail hunter 10 seasons, hunting in prime blacktail country in the mountains of the West Coast, to see the light and admit the awful truth. I was unworthy!

A Coastal Columbia blacktail—especially one living in the old growth forest—is insanely difficult. Not only are they small, wary and endowed with superior senses, but the old growth are formidable and rugged. Most clear-thinking hunters only ever hunt these mountain blacktails once before seeking the civilized blacktails that live down in the cultivated valleys and farmlands along the coast.

Of course, there are those hunters who prefer the high adventure of an old growth forest, mountain blacktail hunt. I know because I used to be one of those nut-cases. Or I used to be until about mid-morning of my first blacktail hunt on Vancouver Island, British Columbia, home to one of the only true breeding, insular populations of Columbia black-tailed deer in North America. The lines drawn between blacktail and mule deer ranges on the mainland of British Columbia, Washington, Oregon and California are manmade and, unfortunately, cross-breeding between mule deer and black-tailed deer occurs everywhere along that border.

All of this was far from my mind on that first blacktail hunt in the mountains of Vancouver Island, mostly because I was freezing. When the wind-driven, slushy rain plastered against my already soaking wet body I hardly noticed. "Just put your foot in front of the other one," I told myself. One step and then another. Whatever you do, don't stop because if you do, it'll be human icicle time.

I have always found the fear of dying to be a great motivator. Unfortunately, it also brings on a wave of self-recriminations. That particular instant was no different. Somehow the chance of taking an old growth forest, mountain blacktail at the risk of a hypothermic death just didn't seem like such a good idea anymore.

My hunting partner, having lived his life on Vancouver Island, had warned me before we climbed the mountain. "Wear your wool pants," he said. "Take a jacket," he said. But I didn't listen. I knew better because I was a whitetail hunter, and I've hunted deer in minus 40 weather in Saskatchewan lots of times.

"Yeah, but you don't get wet," he said.

We'd walked nearly to the top of the mountain on a logging road earlier that morning in the sunshine. But when we left the logged off area—the "slash"—and entered the cathedral-like opening into the old growth timber the whole world changed. Someone told me once that you never forget the first time you set foot into a coastal old growth forest. He was right. The ferns and the moss closed in on me. Everything was suddenly damp and dark. I felt the first chill run down my spine. I also felt the

"Farmland" blacktails aren't considered true Columbia blacktails by those hunters who pursue them in the Northwest's rainforest jungles.

first drop of rain.

When we reached the top of the mountain, my partner pointed down and said, "You go over that edge, and I'll go over this one. When you hit the second growth, cut back across the mountain until you hit the logging road. I'll meet you back at the truck."

I turned to look over the edge where I was supposed to go. I figured that there had to be some kind of mistake; it was almost straight down. I took a tentative step over the edge and was instantly on my back, hanging onto a branch of a slippery shrub that my partner had called "salal." Carefully rolling over, I managed to find a toe-hold. By backing most of the way down and hanging on to whatever purchase my numbed fingers could find, I slowly hunted my way down through the old growth.

Well, to say that I "hunted" the old growth might be exaggerating. In fact to even say that my descent was controlled would be exaggerating, but I did finally manage to make my way to the second growth. Thankfully, the slippery salal

Ultimate Big Game Adventures

thinned out, only to be replaced, to my horror, with a nasty, spiny plant they call "devil's club." I also realized that the hunt was rapidly turning into an ordeal. The rain turned to sleet by the time that I managed to cross the last ravine between myself and the logging road. About then, the clouds rolled right down the mountainside to blot out my vision.

One step and then another. Zombie-like I trudged downward. There was a moment of real fear when I began to wonder if I was heading in the right direction. The slush was plastered an inch thick against my thin cotton clothing by then, and I actually stopped and considered turning around. Luckily my mind was still functioning well enough to remember the old plumber's saying about there being only two things that run downhill. Hypothermic hunters are the third.

Five minutes later, after I rounded a switchback, I saw the truck. I was saved! Once I realized this, my thoughts turned to my partner's safety. He must have been caught in the blizzard as I had been. What if he never made it off the mountain? Brave man that I was, I knew that I would have to go back up the mountain to find him. Being a reasonable brave man, though, I decided that spring would be a good time to do so. After all, it would be easier to find his body when the snow melted.

As I got closer to the truck, I realized that it was running. Through the fogged window I recognized my partner.

"You made it!" I said as I opened the door.

"Made what?" he asked.

I didn't answer because I was too busy trying to change into my dry street clothes. Dressed in the dry stuff, I pulled myself into the cab and planted my frozen hands over the vent. Believing that my partner had barely survived the ordeal, I expected him to turn the vehicle around and head for the nearest warm bath. Instead, he pulled out his lunch.

"Where do you want to hunt this afternoon?" he asked.

"What did you say?" I asked, looking at him like he was out of his gourd.

"Where do you want to hunt this afternoon?" he repeated.

Then and there I knew that I had made two

This mass of Columbia blacktail antlers bears witness to the fabulous deer hunting offered by Arrow Five Outfitters near Zenia, California.

hunting trips for old growth forest Columbia blacktails — my first and last.

For months after that hunt I shuddered when anyone mentioned old growth forest. But shuddering when anyone mentioned old growth was not nearly as bad as convulsing when anyone mentioned blacktails. Unless I got some professional help, I'd never hang my tag on a big Columbia black-tailed deer.

OREGON OR BUST

Fortunately for all us "outclassed" old growth forest blacktail hunters, there are outfitters (masochists) who specialize in guiding for Columbia blacktails. Once I accepted that I had a problem and needed help, the road to recovering my self esteem was obvious, it started with a call to Doug Gattis, owner of Southern Oregon Game Busters, to book a hunt. Unfortunately, the first time, I made the mistake of scheduling the blacktail hunt with Doug right after my Saskatchewan whitetail season and ran into

Spotting a Columbia blacktail in the California hills takes plenty of practice.

technical difficulties and couldn't make it (orders from my wife, she seemed to think that four straight months of hunting was enough).

Needless to say, that year, Doug's hunters killed several monster blacktails in the 140 Boone and Crockett class. Needless to say, I had high hopes of similar success when I rebooked the hunt for the next year. Or I did until I stepped off the airplane in Medford, Oregon, and had my hopes broiled away by a blazing sun that was doing its best to turn the coastal rainforests of Oregon into the Sahara Desert. It was pretty evident that even with Doug's professional help, my odds of killing a camel were better than my odds of tagging a trophy blacktail.

In spite of the fact that we still-hunted our way up and down some of the most beautiful country to be found at the epicenter of the global warming trend, I didn't touch the trigger of my Knight muzzleloader. Doug showed me dozens of deer, none of which were willing to become blacktail burgers. And none of which were as large as the nine or 10 huge black-tailed bucks that we saw every day hanging around

Doug's house! I even remember some of their names—Bucky, Eye-guard, Big Boy and the Psycho Twins. They walked around in the middle of the day, posing for my video camera, safe as babies, because … why? It suddenly occurred to me to ask the obvious question.

"Doug?" I asked nicely while peering through my viewfinder.

"Yes?" Doug answered.

"Is it legal to hunt right here in your backyard?"

"Yep. Go ahead if you want," He said. "Never could shoot a buck with a name myself."

In spite of knowing that the bucks were taking unfair advantage of the hunting ethic, neither could I.

TRAIL LEADS FARTHER SOUTH

Busted by the unseasonably warm weather in Oregon, and humbled once again by the black-tailed deer's ability to do whatever it takes to

     Ultimate Big Game Adventures

Tina Marie Schaafsma of Arrow Five Outfitters helped the author find this great buck.

survive the hunting season, including hiding out in a blacktail outfitter's backyard, I was still badly in need of professional help. Naturally I sought out the man behind the name that continually crops up in Columbia backtail hunting circles—Jim Schaafsma, owner of Arrow Five Outfitters. Jim and his wife, Tina Marie, live in Columbia black-tailed deer heaven near Zenia, a small town in northern California. Their hunters take some awesome blacktails—true blacktails recognized by the Boone and Crockett Club. I'd hunted Coues' deer with the Schaafsma's in Old Mexico before and felt that I knew them well enough to request a little help.

"Please! You gotta help me! Please!" I wouldn't call it begging exactly, more like asking in a pleading manner … from a groveling position on my knees.

Before you can say, "load up the truck and head to Beverly," I was on my way to the Schaafsma ranch to hunt huge Columbia blacktails.

"There's one," Tina Marie said, looking through her binoculars. "Under that live oak across the valley."

"Sure is," Jim agreed.

"Right, I see it," I said. … But, I didn't see it.

"There's another buck just under the ridge," Jim added.

"Uh huh. See it too," Tina Marie confirmed.

"Yep. Got it." I hadn't got it.

"Big one! Lying in the shade down the trail, near the creek!" Jim exclaimed.

"Nice one all right," Tina Marie said.

"Down the trail?" I poured over the landscape, searching for something, anything that looked like a deer, and didn't see a thing.

That first day taught me a valuable lesson about Columbia black-tailed deer hunting, the little son-of-a-guns are hard to see! Tina Marie and Jim spotted them by the dozen, literally, while I got blisters on my eyeballs trying to find even one. By the end of the day they'd spotted 30 different bucks, and I'd spotted one. On day two I started to get the knack of picking the deer out of the shadows and by day three I was

At left, the author with one of his first true-blooded Columbia blacktails taken on Vancouver Island, British Columbia. Wanting to torture himself some more, he later traveled to Oregon and California in pursuit of trophy blacktails. Far right and center, are the results of hunts consecutive seasons in northern California.

all over the little rascals.

Each day we'd head into the hills and glass for rutting bucks. When we would spot a big-enough buck, we'd make a stalk on it. We saw an average of 35 bucks per day with a high of 50 different bucks on one day! But, unfortunately, things didn't go my way. One large buck that Jim had been seeing every day prior to my arrival, disappeared the day I got there. Another huge buck was swallowed up by a freak fog bank one morning and at least three others disappeared seconds before I was about to pull the trigger.

I'd spend the middle of the day still-hunting and then would hit the binoculars with the Schaafsma's again in the late afternoon. It finally happened on the last day. A monster of a 4x4 stood up from its bed as I still-hunted through the white oak forest. Although neither Jim nor Tina Marie were there right then to help me judge it, there was no doubt that it was a world record for sure—far bigger than any blacktail

that I'd ever sneaked up on in 10 years of hunting them. In one motion I lifted my Knight muzzleloader and fired. The buck dropped in its tracks, but as I walked up to it, right before my very eyes, I witnessed it "shape change" into a somewhat smaller buck!

The good news was that I was thrilled because the buck was still larger by far than any other Columbia blacktail that I'd ever taken. The bad news was, since I knew there were much larger bucks on the ranch, I needed to figure out a way to come back the next year. The other good news was, I hadn't forgotten how to "ask in a pleading manner."

"Please! Can I come back? Please?"

IF AT FIRST YOU DON'T SUCCEED ...

Before you can say "loaded up the family and headed back down to Beverly," I was back on the Schaafsma's ranch, this time avec my entire family. The pictures that I'd taken the

year before, showing the Schaafsma's quaint antler clad lodge, tucked in a shaded corner of the ranch, was enough to convince the crew that they should accompany me for a late-August hunt. After the 20-hour drive, as soon as we opened the doors and greeted Schaafsma's, my family scattered. My son went to look for lizards, my daughter to follow a wild pig family across the yard, my wife to the veranda. I headed into the golden hills to look for a bigger blacktail than the one that I'd taken the year before.

"There he is," Tina Marie said. We hadn't been gone from the ranch house and my family for more than an hour when Tina Marie spotted the first buck.

"Yep. You bet. I see him." … I didn't see him.

"He's shed his velvet since this morning," Jim added after checking the buck out more closely. "You ready to shoot so early in your hunt?"

Ready to shoot? Was Jim serious? After all the years that I'd spent trying to find a really big

blacktail, was I ready to shoot? Hell yes! I was ready to crawl across a mile of broken glass in the first second of the hunt if that's what I had to do!

The buck was the same buck that they'd seen for several days in a row, bedding along a low ridge in the valley. In August, Tina Marie explained, the black-tailed bucks tend to stay put in one spot or very close to it. That very morning Tina Marie had seen the big 5x4 again while scouting. It had been in full velvet then, but now, as we worked our way closer and I could actually see the buck, it was obvious that the buck was "hard-horned." Its antlers shone like polished mahogany in the mid-afternoon sun.

BOOM! For the second year in a row, I aimed at a big California blacktail and touched the trigger of my muzzleloader, sending the bullet on its devastating way. Five minutes later, after all the years of trying, I finally held in my hands the toughest of the deer to hunt, a big, mature Columbia black-tailed buck. ■

CHAPTER FIFTEEN:

WHITE MANES & BLACK-POWDER

Judging caribou isn't easy.

The white-maned caribou bull that we'd seen from nearly a mile away an hour earlier, was now standing much closer, within muzzleloader distance ... I hoped. My Dene Indian guide Ricky Drygeese and I poked our heads over the lichen-covered boulder that we'd used for cover during the stalk. The bull glared intently at our hiding place.

"Ricky!" I said urgently. "What do you think? 125?"

"No ... more." Ricky's voice remained calm, typical of his people.

I raised the Knight rifle, rested it on top of the boulder and then fixed the caribou bull firmly in the crosshairs. "OK, what do you think? 150?" I asked, my thumb poised against the safety. All I needed was confirmation from my guide, and the 310-grain slug would be on its devastating way.

"No ... more," Ricky replied, shaking his head. "He has good bez."

"Bez?!" I asked anxiously. "What then," I pressed, "170?"

"No ... 300." Ricky said stoically. "Maybe more."

Now, being an outfitter myself, I know that the worst clients to guide are other outfitters and outdoor writers. They (we) know everything. I was trying to be a good boy.

"Ricky," I said matter-of-factly. "If that bull is more than 175 yards away, I'll eat my hat."

Ricky ignored my challenge, keeping his eyes glued to his binoculars. "He's got a spike for his second shovel, good first shovel, weak tops and no back-scratchers," he said, lowering his binoculars. "He'll score over 325."

Hiding behind that boulder, out there in the vast, open tundra of the Northwest Territories, I'd just learned an important lesson on how to hunt Central Canada barren ground caribou. When you've dreamed about it for 30 years, planned it for months, taken 10 days off of work to do it, driven all the way up to Yellowknife, flown in a twin Otter several

hundred miles, ridden in an aluminum skiff for several days and walked for several dozen miles, the last thing you want to do is shoot an average bull caribou.

Conversely, the first thing you want to do is judge the antler size of the caribou bull. Then you judge the distance.

"We can do better," Ricky said confidently. "He won't make Boone and Crockett."

The white-maned caribou was understandably growing tired of us talking about whether he should be killed. As he turned and started walking away, I weighed the factors. Since I first read about hunting caribou 30 years before, I'd dreamed about it. Now I was staring at a respectable bull walking away from me. Better than that, the bull was within muzzleloader range—or he used to be. By the time I decided that I wanted the bull, he was a good 50 yards farther.

"I want him, Ricky," I said, clicking off the safety. "How far now?"

"One-seventy-five," Ricky replied, as he reached over and stopped me from pulling the pin on the moving bull. "He'll stop."

Three more steps and the bull, as if on command, stopped and turned broadside. Maybe he saw the puff of smoke and heard the boom, but I doubt it. He collapsed instantly when the big bullet hit him square and tight behind the shoulder.

CARIBOU CHARACTERISTICS

Central barren ground caribou are the second smallest species recognized by most record books. In order of comparison, antler-wise, the barren ground, Quebec-Labrador and mountain caribou varieties are all larger. Only the woodland caribou is smaller.

Antler size, though, is relative. Any caribou bull worth his salt will have antlers that would make the largest whitetail look stunted. Only a moose or a monster elk can compare in the antler department and only then if you don't compare body size. A caribou bull of any species will have antlers that appear out-sized for its body.

Speaking of body size, when I stepped off the 176 paces to my fallen bull, even though I knew what to expect, I was shocked at just how small a mature caribou is. I've killed white-tailed bucks that were at least as heavy. A caribou is shaped differently, though, sporting a larger head and belly and a smaller front and back end. On the hoof, I'd be surprised if my bull topped 300 pounds. The larger caribou species reputedly hit 500 pounds and, in extreme cases, have been reported up to 1,000 pounds.

All of these caribou facts might have been important, but the one that most interested me, now that I had my bull down, was what the heck caribou meat tasted like. I asked Ricky this as he skinned and quartered the bull; taking less time than it takes to tell it. As he cut a rack of ribs for our shore lunch, he told me that caribou was his family's staple winter food—his way of saying caribou tastes better than moose.

Fred Webb's Courageous Lake camp served as the base of operations for the author and his father during their Central Canada barren ground caribou operaion.

"It's a fat one. Good," Ricky said as he carefully cut a thick strip of fat from each side of the bull's back. "This I'll dry by the stove and eat with jerky."

"You mean not even cook it?" I asked, eyeing the layer of fat.

Ricky didn't answer, reaching into the body cavity for the kidneys.

"I'll boil these tonight," he said, holding the giblets up for me to see. "You can try them."

"Yummy," I said, not too convincingly. "I'll pass on the fat, though."

In no time we had the bull loaded into our packs and were heading back to the lake shore where we'd left our aluminum skiff. As we walked, caribou drifted past. These smaller bulls, cows and calves paid little attention to us, hardly stopping to look before continuing their fall migration.

COURAGEOUS LAKE

We were hunting on the shores of Courageous Lake, just south of the Arctic Circle, and even though it was August, the caribou were around the lake in abundance. In spite of what I thought were large numbers of caribou, we were seeing just the leading edge of the greater herd still on its way. Within the month, if we stayed, the hundreds of caribou we were seeing daily would increase to thousands.

My father and I had driven up to the Territories and arrived a day early in Yellowknife, situated on the edge of the tundra. Naturally, we asked directions to the nearest sporting goods store, hoping to get the inside scoop.

Dale Johnston, owner of Yellowknife's Wolverine Sports Shop, was more than helpful, confirming what we already knew about the outfitters we'd hired—Fred Webb and his son, Martin. They were true professionals and would certainly put us onto caribou, Dale said. If we had time, Dale suggested that we drop a

fishing line in Courageous Lake. Lake trout, he explained, teemed in the lake and would be feeding voraciously on anything that moved. He told us that we could expect fish in the 20-pound range and reasonably hope for the odd 30-pounder.

During the winter an ice road crosses the tundra, but during the summer, the only way across is by air. As we flew in the twin Otter, the land for as far as I could see looked like brown Swiss cheese with all the holes filled with water.

The first thing I saw upon deplaning, was a caribou. The young bull stood up behind camp on a ridge. Fred was there waiting to greet us. There was no doubt that he was a man more at home on an ice flow than in a big city. It's hard to say if I was more excited about meeting Fred in person or about the hunt itself. Since I was a youngster old enough to read my first hunting magazine, I'd known of Fred.

Fred's camp turned out to be comfortable and beautifully situated right on the sandy shores of Courageous Lake. Over a fine meal that evening, I mentioned to Fred that I'd be hunting with a muzzleloader, and he immediately put to bed any fears that I might have had about using a smokepole. He told me that if I

could shoot accurately, I wouldn't have any trouble filling both my caribou tags. He also mentioned that there was a reasonable chance of taking a wolverine or wolf on the trip. I held tags for both.

FATHER-SON ADVENTURE

Sleep came slowly that first night. Or at least it came slowly to me. Dad was snoring a storm within minutes of official lights-out time and he was still snoring when Martin fired up the camp generator early the next morning. In spite of my anticipation, neither my father nor I had a caribou in the boat when we returned to camp well before dark that first day. Yet, we were close to vast numbers of the migrating beasts.

Our guides had made it clear that we should hold out for a record-book caribou, and we did, too—at least we did until dinner that first night. That's when one of the other hunters in camp mentioned that there was a bull standing behind camp. My father is a meat-hunter from way back and spending a whole day letting all those tasty caribou walk away was just too much for the old guy. Within the minute he was leaning against the guide's shack, training his trusty and ancient .270 on the bull.

The author's father, Hal, is an avid hunter who honed his skill on Saskatchewan whitetails. At left, he took a great bull that stayed outside of muzzleloader range for the author. Far right, the author with the bull that he just couldn't resist after dreaming for so long about the majestic, white-maned creatures.

At the shot, the bull dropped. It was lying exactly 110 yards away from the kitchen, perfect as far as my father was concerned. The bull didn't have record-book headgear, but it did have those desirable double shovels that experienced caribou hunters look for.

The next day was a repeat of the first—lots of caribou, but nothing Boone and Crockett class. The difference between the first day and the second day was that the guides kept a close eye on my father, stopping him from shooting another relatively small caribou.

The third day started much the same way, except this time we spotted a huge bull making its way along the shoreline. The waves were high that day, driven to unnerving heights by gale force winds pounding across the tundra. Expertly, our guides beached the boats, leaving my father and I free to dash toward the bull on what we hoped would be an intercept course.

We judged the angle well, but even at the closest point, the bull was too far to attempt a shot with my muzzleloader. Too far for me, but just within maximum range for my father. He shot three times, connecting twice. The caribou took less than 10 steps from where it had been standing at the first shot. The bull turned out to be every bit as big as it had looked when we first saw it. A true giant, it easily made the top half of the Boone and Crockett record book listings.

On the fourth day I killed my first caribou bull, the one that I described stalking and killing at the beginning of the story. A beautiful animal by any measure, I was soon to find out that my caribou offered great eating to boot. Ricky had his small cook stove fired up and was roasting ribs by the time that I dropped the heavy antlers, cape and front quarters into the boat. He asked if I might want to spend a few minutes catching grayling in a nearby creek, but I declined.

I didn't want to do anything but sit there on the shores of Courageous Lake, smell roasting caribou meat and watch all of those magnificent white-maned bulls stream across the tundra. While I sat there, it occurred to me that the reality of hunting caribou exceeds the dream. ■

CHAPTER SIXTEEN:

NORD BY NORTHEAST

The first hunt started with a phone call to Newfoundland.

"Hi, I heard you guys take the biggest woodland caribou in the world," I said.

"Yawedowhadcanidoforya?" came the reply.

"I'm sorry. I was trying to reach Don Tremblett of Mount Peyton Outfitters out in Newfoundland, Canada. Where'd I call anyway? Someplace in Iceland?" I asked.

"Yerspeakintoim," said the guy on the other end.

"Gee, never heard of Yerspeakintoim! Is that near Afghanistan?" I asked.

"Wallgetthacrudoddayerearsbay!" came the reply.

"Ya, well same to you pal! Anybody speekee Englishhee there?" I asked hopefully.

The phone went silent for a second before the voice came back on again.

"Ya-then-what-say-we-start-over-bay?" the man said a bit more slowly and clearly.

"Hey, wow! English! I thought you were speaking Lebanese or something! Listen, I'm trying to book a woodland caribou hunt with Mount Peyton Outfitters. I hear they're the best. Do you know a fellow by the name of Don Tremblett?" I asked.

"Ya-this-is-him-you-were-speaking-to. We-has-us-a-peculiar-accent-out-here," he said.

Peculiar? Lobster dory to that! Peculiar accents are at least understandable, but hard "Out Port" accents pouring forth at full speed from the mouth of a real live Newfoundland "Bay Man," are about as understandable as codfish gibberish!

Now for those who don't know, Out Ports are the port villages that exist along the remote outer coast of the island of Newfoundland. Bay Men, as I understand it, are the country folk who inhabit the wild places that the "Townies" don't. And Don Tremblett, is a Newfoundland Bay Man. Tough, like the North Atlantic weather. Big, like the land the residents affectionately call "The Rock" and hardy, like the wind-bitten conifers that grow thick from the solid granite.

Over the few hundred years that they've inhabited this harsh eastern coast of Canada, the

Newfoundland Out Port people, like Don, have developed a language that resembles English when spoken, but isn't understandable by the rest of us North Americans until it's slowed down below warp speed. Fortunately, there exists a common reason for making the effort to understand each other; a reason for Newfoundlanders to slow their speech and for the rest of us with a passion for hunting to speed up our brains. Woodland caribou. Big woodland caribou.

Newfoundland is the only place you can hunt woodland caribou, and the government officials with Tourism Newfoundland & Labrador have been helping put area outfitters on the map. They know that, eventually, every hunter intent on completing a caribou slam, (taking each of the five varieties of caribou), and every hunter interested in completing the Super Slam, (taking each of the North American big game species) must show up on the "Rock." Among the caribou cognoscenti, the Mount Peyton area is synonymous with giant bulls. It's one of the best places to hunt woodland caribou, the smallest-antlered of the caribou varieties recognized by Boone and Crockett.

For years I'd thought about the hunt, but never booked. It wasn't until I learned of Don Tremblett's incredible success at guiding his clients to monster woodland caribou that I made the effort to pick up the phone. Little did I know that I'd need an interpreter! Fortunately, I wasn't the first hunter unable to decipher Don's cryptic language, so he slowed up. And before a Newfoundlander can recite "War and Peace" from cover to cover 10 times, I had my hunt booked with the legendary caribou outfitter.

BONJOUR, CA VA BIEN?

The phone never left my ear; I simply dialed another number. The Newfoundland hunt was to take place during the first 10 days of October, and the way I had it figured, that left 20 empty days before whitetail season in Saskatchewan. Since I was going to be all the way to the other side of the continent, I might as well detour through "nord-ern" Quebec for a Quebec-Labrador caribou hunt. Right?

"Bonjour," someone answered.

"Bon jer. J ma pell Jim. Jess swee lookee poor grandee caribooee sont chassee moi!" I said. In spite of passing 10th grade French with a 51 percent average, I was amazed at how easily it all came back. "Quesk a vooz alley dits don la sall dee class dee o jourd wee?"

Unlike Don Tremblett out in Newfoundland, Siegfried Gagnon, my contact with Tourism Quebec at the time, spoke English.

"Ahh, Monsieur Shockey! Glad to hear you're working on your French!" he said sarcastically. Siegfried and I had spoken several times over the years about coming out to the "Fleur de lis" province for a Quebec-Labrador caribou hunt. These caribou are one of the largest-antlered of the caribou varieties, but finding those "largest-antlered" bulls ain't easy. Or it isn't unless you have inside information.

Enter Peter Palmer, head honcho for Nunami Outfitters. He's been outfitting for caribou all over Quebec for more than 20 years, but in the two years before my hunt he'd been lighting up the record books with monster bulls. He operates out of a four-season camp located on the

eastern side of Hudson Bay, two hours north by plane from La Grande, Quebec. The operative words here are "four-season camp." Peter is able to take hunters out during late October when the 200,000 or so caribou that make up the Leaf River Herd are in full "gimme lovin'" rut!

"Hey Siegfried, what'cha doing in late October?" I asked.

And so, as simple as "uh, doo, twaw," Siegfried and I worked out the details and arranged the hunt. We'd meet in Montreal on the 20th of October.

THE-STAGS-WAZ-IN-THE-BOGS

Six months and about 12 hours of flying time later, I stepped into the Gander, Newfoundland airport.

"Hey you'll never believe it, but everybody in this place speaks funny!" I said, reaching out my hand to shake the big callused mitt extended to me. "I thought it was just you!"

"Don't-be-makin'-no-fun-of-us-lads-from-Newfoundland-now," Don's laughing eyes said just the opposite. The more fun the better. "We-saved-a-special-room-fer-you."

The trip from the Gander airport to Don's lodge passed in a blur of misunderstandings, "pardon me's" and "sorry I didn't quite catch that's," but I did manage to gather that the season had been going well to that point. The biggest bull from the week before scored 340 B&C points—a monster that would place near the top of the record book. Better news than that, though, if I was interpreting Don's words correctly, was that the "stags-waz-in-the-bogs!" This was a good thing

because "stags-in-the-bogs" meant they were rutting. And that meant big bulls.

We arrived in camp late, midnight or so, and since I was bagged from traveling all the way across Canada, I opted not to have a nip of something called "Screech," whatever that was, and headed directly to my "special room." The rest of the hunters and guides, awaiting the morrow's hunt were already counting sheep in various wings of the large and beautiful Mount Peyton lodge situated on the shores of a pristine lake.

My head had just touched the pillow when "it" started.

ROARRRTHHHOOINK!!! I nearly dislocated my neck jumping from the bed. F-18 flying through the room? Earthquake? I shook my fuzzy head clear. No, the sound was too loud. Volcano? I'd almost settled on this as the obvious answer when "it" happened again. ROARRRTHHHOOINK!!! Hail Mary full of grace … the world was ending! The walls shook. "It," it turned out, was a guide by the name of Roy snoring in the room next to my special room.

"Haveagoodsleepbay?" Don's bearded smiling face was the first thing my crusted red eyes focused on five hours later.

"Huh?"

"He-wants-to-know-how-ya-slept." Another smiling face leapt into focus, and then another and another. The main room of the lodge was chocker block full of hunters and Bay Men. All smiling, most laughing out loud.

"Kindaloudthenwasee?" Don roared. "Savedyathespecialroomalrighthahahaha."

"Hahahahahahahaha." It was the sound, I quickly learned, that Bay Men like to make the most. "Hahahahahahahaha."

WORLD RECORD STAG

After breakfast, hunters and guides paired up, jumped on quads and disappeared into the North Atlantic mist. My guide, Todd Gillingham, and I were headed for the bogs.

"There's-a-stag," Todd said, peering through his binoculars. "Andanotherthereandtherewegottago."

"Whoa, slow down. Say again?" I said, trying to pick out the caribou.

"One'll-go-over-300," Todd said, motioning urgently for me to follow him.

Bog. Slurp. Glurp. Every step was an effort as my boots and the bog made love; only the vision of that 300-point caribou in the distance kept my legs pumping. The minimum score for a woodland caribou to qualify for the B&C record book is 295. More importantly to me, according to the Longhunter Society record book, the muzzleloading world record for woodland caribou at the time was a monster bull scoring 299⅞ B&C points, taken in 1994 by Collins Kellogg, Sr. The bull out in the bog was larger, much larger. Slurp. Blurp. Glurp.

As we closed the distance, it became apparent that, in fact, the bog was crawling with caribou, at least 40 that we could count. There were more feeding on the "barrony knobs," moss-covered bumps rising here and there above the muskeg bog. At 200 yards, the big bull lifted his head and seemed to notice us.

"Holdstill!" Todd ordered.

But it wasn't us that he was interested in; another lesser bull appeared out of the scrub trees to our right. For a second the two bulls looked at each other and then charged! Wham! They hit hard, crashing antler against antler. A point broke off and flipped through the air. Damn! Wait! From the smaller bull! Good!

"Quick, I have to get closer!" I said.

Todd started toward the battling bulls, ignoring the cows that instantly picked us out.

Wham! Wham! The bulls were locked in four-wheel-drive, head to head.

"How far?" I asked, readying my Knight muzzleloader.

Todd hit the larger bull with the rangefinder. "Eighdyards."

Suddenly the larger bull seemed to notice the 30-odd cows standing at full attention and pulled away from the fight. BOOM! It was too late. The 300-grain Swift bullet was already on its way. Sixty days later the bull was officially scored at 308 B&C points, eclipsing the former world record. Interestingly, that day, all the caribou hunters in camp scored on big bulls, as did two of the moose hunters. The next morning, the rest of the moose hunters tagged up. One week later, a hunter from the next group killed a woodland caribou that scored 359⅛ B&C points—the sixth largest woodland caribou ever taken at the time and the largest taken since 1966.

But I was in Quebec by then.

CARIBOU BY THE THOUSANDS

Siegfried and I met in Montreal and then connected to La Grande, the site of the hydroelectric project to end all hydroelectric projects. From there we hopped aboard a speedy looking, amphib Cessna Caravan. As we flew north, past James Bay, I began to notice odd trails cutting here and there across the land, 3,000 feet below. Not only odd because they seemed to stretch from one side of the world to the other, but odd because they were moving!

Peter Palmer's Nunami Outfitters camp is about the biggest, best-equipped North Country camp I've ever had the pleasure of residing in. Peter informed me that it was originally an experimental hydroelectric camp that the Inuit purchased from the government. Located on the shores of a vast water system, Peter's early fall hunters use boats to move about. As late as we were, and as cold as it was, boat travel across the partially frozen lake was problematic. Instead, we'd be heading out by floatplane and would be landing on remote lakes at lower elevations; from those lakes, we'd be hiking inland and upland to try and intercept the caribou migration.

"That one! No that one! No … that one!" I pivoted around, looking at the first bull, then the second and finally the third, the trigger of my

Knight muzzleloader was burning a hole in my finger. "No, wait! Here comes another bull … make that six more! Forget those ones, look over there at those two! Wait, that's not two, that's one giant one!"

In a word, whether you were actually there or simply reading these words about it, the caribou hunt with Nunami Outfitters was "unbelievable." The four hunters in camp the week before our hunt took seven B&C record-book caribou! I took another on the first day of our hunt, a bull that officially scored 376⅝ B&C points, the third largest ever taken with a muzzleloader. I also took my second bull on the first day, but it didn't quite make the all-time book. Call it poor fire control. There were so many bull caribou passing by that my brain locked.

In all, on the first day, I believe that there were more than 2,000 different caribou within range of my Knight muzzleloader. Since I was tagged up, on the second and third day, I went out to video Siegfried and a few of the guides while they hunted for their own caribou. Interestingly, they didn't use the airplane; they couldn't, visibility dropped to near zero when a bank of ice fog from Hudson Bay rolled in. Instead they boarded a huge A-Star helicopter to travel to the caribou hunting ground!

While it might not seem huge by caribou standards, this woodland stag is a whopper.

The helicopter would drop the hunters off in the treeless high country and then head back to camp. The hunters, with Yours Truly in tow, would then hike down to the trees and head cross country until they began to find caribou tracks. We zigged when we should have zagged a few times and had to climb back up above treeline to try and spot where the caribou had gone. But in spite of the downtime, conservatively speaking, we saw at least 1,500 different bulls over the next two days. Everyone tagged up on great bulls, and I got some spectacular video footage.

Siegfried was the most selective of the bunch waiting until the last few minutes to take his two bulls. With the day winding down and everyone else done, he made two spectacular shots with his Knight muzzleloader. The "thump" of the bullet hitting the last bull nearly joined the "thup thup thup" of the A-Star returning to pick everyone up. Peter shot a flare into the dying light, to guide the big bird to the nearest landing area. Truly, this hunt is one that every hunter should try to experience at least once. C'est une excellentee adventuree!

Oh revoir.

CHAPTER SEVENTEEN:
DIARY OF A YUKON ODYSSEY

September 13, 2000—I'm driving in the pre-94 Mighty Dodge, heading north on a 1,500-mile drive to Mayo, a small town 200 miles north of Whitehorse, the capital of the Yukon Territories. Got my Thermos of coffee, got my Shania Twain cassette for company, and the weather is gorgeous. Plan to drive as far as I can tonight, sleep in the truck and continue on tomorrow. The floatplane is scheduled to leave from Mayo in 48 hours. If it doesn't leave without me, I'll be hunting for Dall sheep, barren ground caribou, Alaska-Yukon moose and grizzly bear with Richard Rodger, owner of Bonnet Plume Outfitting.

September 14—I'm on gravel now, 100 miles north of the Indian village of Kitwanga. Whitehorse is still a dozen hours away. I drove until 1:30 a.m. last night (today) and slept in the truck for three hours and have been driving ever since. Expect to see a black bear or two on this portion of the road. I'm in sheep country now, too. The weather is ugly. Feel sorry for the guys backpacking up on the sheep mountains.

September 15—In the Yukon now; it's a beautiful day, the poplars are golden here, very pretty.

Got to Mayo 20 minutes before the twin Otter took off. Met the other three hunters—good guys from New Jersey—and jumped on the plane. Flew to MacKlusky Lake, a 45-minute flight. Richard Rodger was there with his blue Super Cub on floats. We loaded up my gear and took off, headed for Kiwi Lake. If the flight in the Otter was breathtaking, this flight in the Cub was almost indescribable, snowcapped mountains on each side, river below, truly the hinterlands. Landed in a glittering lake and met my guides, Mike Oleshak and Stuart Young. They pointed out a bull moose across the lake 300 yards away! Big, but not a taker. Began organizing gear for the hike to spike camp.

September 16—Woke up in the dark. Mike's making coffee on the wood stove. We had bacon and eggs for breakfast, loaded up and started hiking. The boots to wear up here are gum-boots with liners inside. Muskeg bog for two miles and then moose trail. Covered nine or 10 miles today. Found a camp spot and had just unloaded our backpacks when we noticed a herd of 40 caribou two miles farther up the valley. At least 15 good bulls. Stalked them for an hour. Closest bull looked to be a whopper.

The bull was on the edge of a hill, and I couldn't see his whole body, just half of it. As soon as I had a clear shot, I touched the trigger of my Knight muzzleloader. The bull turned and ran, hit hard. That's when we noticed that he only had one antler! What can you do? I felt bad, wouldn't have shot had I known. On the bright side, it'll make for some good eating. We'll come back tomorrow to get all the meat. No fire up here in the alpine; there's no wood. We cooked up some noodles on the tiny backpack burner and are headed for bed. Saw one grizzly today, not big. The weather was cool and overcast. Quite a day.

September 17—We woke up this morning to a blizzard and a foot of new snow on the ground. Retrieved the meat. Exhausted. Wore every single thing I had. Snowed all day, and the wind howled. Ate and hit the sack early.

September 18—More snow again this morning. Knee deep now. We're heading back over the height of land toward Kiwi Lake camp. There's firewood just over the pass. We'll carry everything—heavy loads. We'll camp by two tiny lakes that we passed on the way in.

Going is horrible. I'm breaking trail for the others. They're smaller than I am, but their packs are much heavier. Bottom line, they're in better shape.

Got to the lakes. Done in. Have decided to wait out the weather. We're dragging wood to our campsite and will make a fire to dry everything out. I'm soaking wet from the snow and sweat.

Had an excellent meal of barbecued caribou over the open fire. Ate until I was stuffed.

September 19—Clear skies! Mike and I are heading back into the mountains for sheep.

Walked eight miles through snow. Didn't see any rams or any tracks and couldn't go farther. Snow too deep. Found one grizzly and went after him, but he beat us—gone when we got there. Tough day physically. Went after a herd of 28 caribou. Sneaked up to within 229 yards before they made us. Back to the tent at dark. Have a big roaring fire going. Nothing nicer then a warm fire when you're camped in a snow bank.

September 20—The Otter is coming to pick us up in two days. Too late to take another caribou now; no way to get it backpacked to Kiwi in time. And can't get up where the sheep are, so it's time to head back. We have to bring the rest of the caribou with us. Loaded heavy packs first thing in the morning and started walking. Stu is getting sick. Little wonder. Made it back to the camp in the afternoon. Funny how a plywood cabin will lift your spirits!

Mike just looked out the window, and there's a giant bull moose 500 yards from us! Gotta go!

Unbelievable! What a hunt! Huge moose! We had to work past two smaller bulls to get to the bigger bull. Mike called him in. Points all the way around the top, 28 in all. He's a big, beautiful bull. Captured the entire hunt on video, came to within 15 yards! I couldn't shoot because it was coming right at us grunting and slobbering! Mike was whispering to me that it could charge at any time and I kept telling him "to keep the camera rolling!" (I'll tell you a lot more about the moose hunt later in this chapter.)

September 21—We cut up the bull and got the meat down to the dock and were back in the cabin by 2 p.m. We were drinking coffee when I looked out and noticed a grizzly bear at the other end of the lake. We went after him, got within 200 yards. Not sure if he spotted us or smelled the cabin, but he took off running. I didn't get a shot. Winds gusting to 60 miles per hour, horrible conditions. The leaves are blown off the trees now; it's definitely fall. On the

Knee-deep snow when you're carrying your camp on your back is no fun, even when you're hunting. The author trekked dozens of miles during this chilling adventure in search of sheep, caribou, moose and grizzly bear.

lighter side, the wind blew the top and two sides off the outhouse. Makes for a great view.

September 22 — Weather deteriorating. Fogging in and raining hard. Now 1:30 p.m. The Otter was supposed to be here at 11 a.m. Weather getting worse by the minute.

Just sitting here about to drink a cup of coffee when we heard the Otter coming in! Have to go!

Wind horrible, little visibility, but the pilot landed. Too windy to dock, so he beached the huge plane against the shore, in water thigh deep. Two of us held the plane, while one carried meat. Tough to keep the Otter from blowing offshore. Got soaking wet and cold; raining hard. Finally got everything loaded. The pilot is Cam, cucumber cool, top dog. Took off right into the teeth of the fog; I sat in the front seat as co-pilot, couldn't see a darn thing. Some co-pilot, didn't have a clue what Cam was doing! He turned around after lift-off, and I thought he was landing again, but he headed out the other direction, and we cleared the fog after 10 minutes. That's when it got bad, real bumpy.

Landed at main camp beside Cathleen Lake. Richard informed me that Cam said it was one of the worst flights he'd ever had. Even with

seatbelts, we had to hold onto the ceiling to keep from getting hammered around inside the cockpit. Every time we went by a side valley, the plane would hit turbulence, and we'd get pounded. Thankfully, Cathleen Lake is crystal calm. The camp is a big lodge, two stories high with a fire going. Only too happy to hang my soaking clothing up to dry. Steve, the cook, makes the best bannock in the North. We pigged out and dried out. Need the rest.

September 23 — We got up, had breakfast and headed out in a small boat. Stu and I ferried it through a fast-moving, deep creek and then hiked up to an old cat trail. Saw one good bull moose, but no griz or caribou.

I bet the caribou are just over the next mountain. Big country requires big optimism.

Tomorrow I'll be heading into another camp called Johnson's Hole.

September 24 — The New Jersey
hunters are trailing back here to Cathleen Lake today. Between them they have three big bull moose and one caribou. Steve just put a whole big plate full of bannock in front of me. I might have to eat the whole thing, or at least try.

Made it to Johnson's Hole camp. My new guide will be Gord Wagner, looks and talks like Clint Eastwood. Drank coffee and went to sleep.

September 25 — We're heading out to
look for a rogue grizzly bear that chased one of the guides two days ago. The bear almost had the guide when the client shot to save him. Missed the bear at 25 yards and then again at 30 yards. Admitted later that he hadn't even taken his scope covers off! The bear decided not to press the attack. Last night the bear came through camp, circled all around! Guides and wranglers want this rogue griz dead.

Got him! Took some doing, but got him! Spotted the bear and sneaked up. Took three hours to get within 60 yards. Waited an hour for the griz to give me a shot, it kept weaving through the willows around us! Finally made a mistake! Real nice blond and black grizzly; poked its nose through a little opening, and I shot. Had to be quick, shot a little far back. Griz only went 50 yards. Reloaded

my Knight and shot again, and then again to be sure. Actually shot one more time to be even surer. Old guide's rule, "don't take chances with a rogue grizzly." My heart's still pounding hard.

New hunter flew into camp, fellow named Alfred from Germany, 65 years old. Looking for a big moose.

September 26 — Standing here
among the horses, the bells are clanging, and the horses are saddled up ready for the hunt. Snow fell during the night, 3 inches, more higher up. There are wolf tracks within 25 feet of camp today, and yesterday we heard them howling. My horse's name is Pride.

Did a loop around the mountain, rode all day until dark. Saw one big bull moose—probably a 60-incher. Also saw two groups of caribou, nothing big, no bulls, a few tracks. Slow day, but spectacular country. A wild land.

September 27 — Saddled up this
morning and headed out. We got two hours away from camp, and it started snowing and blowing hard. We pulled into a copse of trees and made a fire and sat there all day. Tried to have a nap in the blowing snow, but couldn't do it. Got back and learned that Alfred got his monster moose! Good for him, nice guy. It's snowing again. Not looking good for tomorrow. Need a good night's sleep.

September 28 — Snowing hard again
today. The other guys have gone to retrieve Alfred's moose. Another moose hunter, Tim from Kansas, is trailing in today. Looks like we'll be spending the day in the cabin, zero visibility. Hopefully the weather will get better tomorrow. It's starting to get long now; it's been more than two weeks. Didn't sleep well last night. The snow builds up on the blue tarp roof, ices up and then slides down the side of the cabin. A whole big sheet of ice at a time; it sounds like a giant grizzly dragging its claws across the outside of the cabin.

September 29 — We waited until
noon today for the weather to clear. It looked like it was going to brighten, so we rigged up the horses and went hunting. Got three miles

At left, the author killed the grizzly that literally had the hunters and guides on the run. Last day this great bull fell at just 40 yards.

out from camp, but the wind was absolutely horrendous and so cold. I don't have the right clothing, wasn't expecting this. Temperature below zero with a 30-mph wind, bitter cold.

September 30 — Visibility terrible, bad conditions again. Tried to get into a back drainage but it was a no-go. Still blowing hard, lots of snow, cold, but we'll give it another shot tomorrow. Getting tired. Alfred got a nice bull caribou today.

October 1 — Nothing today. Bumped into another grizzly. Snow so deep that we could hardly go anywhere high. Had to walk the horses down through one pass, very steep. Tomorrow is the last day of the hunt, going to have to try and get to the Wind River. It's the last place we can go look. Been everywhere else, so this will be it.

October 2 — Today's the most beautiful day we've had in more than two weeks. Clear skies, sun is out. Still lots of snow, but relatively warm or at least the sun just makes you feel better. Tim got a huge moose yesterday, 66 inches wide, should score around 220 B&C. We're off, last day and hopefully the best day.

Got my bull caribou! A huge old warrior! Got him up the Wind River valley, at least 2,000 ver-

tical feet above the valley floor. Saw more than 65 caribou and got the oldest bull, no way he would have survived the winter. Tracked him through the snow, across the face of the mountain. Took one 40-yard shot from my Knight to put him down. What a caribou! 31 points with really beautiful tops, will score 400 B&C—great hunt. Unbelievable hunt!

Richard is coming in the Cub for me tomorrow. He'd better hurry, everything is freezing solid. Utterly beautiful as this land is, I don't want to spend a winter here. How do the animals survive? God knows. In the distance I hear the horse bells tinkling, so clear in the cold, the boys of the Bonnet Plume will be trailing out tomorrow, heading home after three months in the mountains. Surrounded by such vastness I'm humbled and, in a way, saddened. The hunt is over.

October 3 — I'm back in the pre-94 Mighty Dodge. This old friend and I have traveled more than 200,000 miles together, but we've never been loaded down with caribou, moose and grizzly at the same time. I'll be home in 48 hours. What a hunt. What a great hunt. I'll be back! ∎

CHAPTER EIGHTEEN:

HE COULD CHARGE AT ANY SECOND!

Yes dear, I know it's been a week since we talked. Yes dear, I wish I could be there helping you raise our two energetic teenage kids. …"

There I was, 3,000 miles from home, standing in a scrub willow flat on the shore of a beautiful, remote Yukon lake, talking to my wife. The rocky crags of the Wernecke Mountain range had me surrounded, a captive held against my spouse's will.

"… Oh about another three weeks, still hunting for a moose and a caribou. No, I didn't know you really needed someone to talk to. Yes, of course, all I ever think about is you. …"

Next to diamonds, satellite phones are among the greatest marriage-saving devices ever invented and, even better, they don't have any side effects; they never cause marriages like diamonds sometimes do.

"… I mean, what else would I think about out here in the middle of this hunting paradise, so far away from my responsibilities as a husband and father … wait, hang on …"

My guide, Mike Oleshak, was running toward me from the tiny cabin frantically pointing at me and mouthing something at the bottom of his lungs. I tried to make out what he was saying.

"… you … moose …" I frowned for a second and then the light blinked on. "Moose!"

Once Mike saw that I understood, he reversed direction back toward the cabin, waving for me to follow, now! And that's exactly what I did.

We'd been backpacking for a week, hunting for sheep and caribou and had only just returned to the cabin a few minutes before. Naturally, as soon as we'd arrived, like the good wayward husband that I am, I'd headed for my satellite phone to call my wife and see how she was coping as a single mother raising two teenagers. Mike, on the other hand, and Stu Young, his second in command, had headed to the roof of the cabin to spot for any moose that might be taking a late afternoon stroll along the lake.

"Big moose!" Mike nearly pushed me up the ladder to the cabin roof where he had his spotting scope set up on a tripod. "He's half-a-mile down the lake with a cow!"

One glimpse was all that I needed to see of the

123

The roof of their Yukon cabin stood testament to the great moose hunting. From here, the author first glimpsed his huge bull.

gigantic bull. As quickly as it takes to tell it, I was down the ladder and grabbing for my Knight muzzleloader.

"The camera! Don't forget the camera!" Stu remembered that I was supposed to be there shooting a hunting video. "Quick!"

Mike was already closing in on the bull, cow-calling like a lovelorn swamp donkey.

We'd covered about 500 yards at double-speed when Mike slowed.

"Damn!" I mouthed what we were both thinking. "What do we do?"

First one small (and I use the term loosely) bull moose stepped out of a scruffy spruce patch that we were keeping between us and the big bull. Then another stepped out. The two young bulls weren't about to try to steal the real Mrs. McCoy away from the big bull, but they must have figured to get a little action from the new, hot-to-trot doll coming their way. The fact that Mike and I, caught out in a wide-open meadow, didn't even remotely resemble a cow moose, didn't seem to phase the young bulls.

They were looking for some lovin' and picky they were not.

"Make a bull moose call!" I suggested. "Maybe it'll scare them off."

Mike turned and gave me a sour "give your head a shake" look. Having a bull moose make love to you might certainly be unpleasant, but having that same bull tromp you into compost because you challenged it to a fight to the death, would be far worse.

"No, we'll wait," Mike said. "Hopefully they won't smell us and spook back by the big bull."

So we waited away the precious minutes of daylight, willing the two young bulls to step out of our way. The young bulls, however, were far more proactive, nonchalantly walking toward us; 100, 80, 60 yards, they closed the distance, grunting as they came. Finally, at 30 yards, the larger of the pair stopped and stared.

Taking a quick break to cast a line in the waters of the remote northern wilderness is a temptation most hunters can't ignore.

BIG ADVENTURE

Now, I don't know if you've ever had the opportunity to look up the nostrils of a very close bull moose, but trust me when I tell you that it's a hairy experience. They're just soooo big! The moose I mean, and they're especially soooo big in the area of the Yukon that I happened to be hunting in—an area owned by Richard Rodger and his partners Curt and Marcia Thompson. Their outfit is Bonnet Plume Outfitters which encompasses 6,000 square miles of the wildest real estate left in North America. I'd hunted Dall sheep in the area years before and after seeing dozens of "hardly (if at all) hunted" monster moose on that trip, it had always been my intention to return.

The moose standing in front of us, young though they were, were members of the largest species of moose, the Alaska-Yukon variety. At

best, the larger of the two sported antlers that might have stretched the tape to 40 inches or so. The big bull we were after was at least a 60-incher, not terribly wide when you're talking a species of moose with antlers that can push 80 inches, but then the bull we were after had all the "fixins." Its antlers had long palms, lots of well-defined points, 14 per side and wide pans; it was a bull that had every chance of qualifying for the B&C record book, provided the two young bulls didn't blow it for the big bull, and us.

The week before, when Richard had flown me to the lake, I'd stood on the steps of the cabin and watched a bull moose tear a 30-foot spruce tree out by the roots and then toss it around for 15 minutes before breaking it in two. According to Richard, the moose wasn't a shooter and was still in its easy-going, pre-rut stage. Right, tell that to the 30-foot tree with the broken back! Just before he taxied away in the Super Cub, Richard assured me that by the time we returned from backpacking, the rut would be in full swing and the big boys would be aggressive and coming to

Success and safety on a wilderness hunt require a good guide and a good pilot. The author had both in the Yukon.

calls. He was right. Unfortunately, the same went for the small bulls.

FIGHTIN' WORDS

UGGFF.

The two young bulls nearly dislocated their thick necks when they whipped around to look and see who'd UGGFF'ed at them.

UGGFF.

The big bull must have decided that he wanted both babes—the droopy-nosed one that he already had and the weird looking, two-headed camouflaged cow out in the meadow.

"He's coming!" Mike exclaimed, taking the camera and shifting behind me. "I'll video."

"I got a better idea," I said. "How about you stand out here in front, and I'll video?!"

Mike didn't respond; there wasn't time.

UGGFF.

The monstrous animal disappeared into a ravine 150 yards away; only his grunting advance kept us posted as to his whereabouts. Seconds later, his rack floated into view 50 yards away. It was a wall of bone and that wall of

bone was coming directly at us!

"Take him!" Mike's urgent whisper was captured forever on the sound track of the video camera.

"I can't! I've got no shot!" My own urgent reply was also captured.

UGGFF.

Closer and closer he swayed through the meadow, displaying 28, polished, hunter-killing spikes—each capable of shishkabobbing Mike and me. If his intention was to make us cower in fear, speaking for myself at least, it worked.

UGGFF.

At 15 yards he stopped, towering over us, slobbering, beady eyes fixed on us. He obviously wasn't amused by our little joke, you know, that "imitating a cow in heat" thing. Mike wasn't packin' heat, and my Knight, filled as it was with only 100 grains of powder and a single 300-grain Nosler bullet, suddenly felt inadequate. Or maybe it was me who felt that way.

The line between being stomped into the tundra and shooting a record-book bull moose is sometimes thin. It has never been thinner for the author than in the Yukon.

Rather than shooting the bull, I was thinking in terms of offering an apology for disturbing him. "Sorry Mr. Enraged Bull Moose, but it was all Mike's idea. He's unarmed by the way, so if you'll just let me back out of here without stomping me into goo. …

"He could charge at any second!" Mike, a true, ice-water-in-the-veins professional, was still running the camera.

"Can't shoot 'til he turns!" I said, still staring dead ahead. "Keep the camera rollin'!"

At the time, it seemed like the standoff lasted 20 minutes. But the video footage of the event puts the actual time of our peril at about two minutes. The bull turned his head toward the two smaller bulls that were watching the show from a safe distance away. The big bull must have decided that they were laughing and needed a thumping because he started to go after them. The first step that he took in their direction was the last step that he ever took without a big Nosler-sized hole in his heart. He didn't go 30 yards before tipping over.

It took us a full day to quarter the moose and then quarter the quarters again. Then it took another half day to hump the moose parts the 500 yards through the swamp to the floatplane dock. Lying in the round, the bull measured an honest 10 feet from nose to tail and 8 feet from hoof to hump! His antlers were officially scored at 222 net B&C points, number two (by only two points), in the muzzleloader record book. Best of all, there wasn't a scrap of meat left on the bones when we were done, every one of the 730 delicious, deboned pounds ended up in my freezer (except the tenderloins, which we had for dinner in the cabin that night).

Oh yeah, I almost forgot, the satellite phone was still sitting on the step by the cabin, exactly where I'd dropped it before the stalk. Take my word for it, an enraged bull moose at 15 yards doesn't hold a candle to an enraged wife at 3,000 miles. ∎

CHAPTER NINETEEN:

BEHIND THE SCENES FOR SHIRAS MOOSE

Camera. Action!

At 80 yards the bull looked huge!

"Now?" I asked Steve Finch, the intrepid Realtree Outdoors cameraman.

"Yeah," Steve said. "Take him." My finger started to squeeze …

"Wait!" Steve whispered. "Not yet! Something's beeping in the background!"

Off in the distance, across the valley, a road construction vehicle was backing up. BEEP, BEEP, BEEP! (Fortunately, the sound of the monster truck beeping beeped out what I was saying.)

"OK. Take him," Steve said, his voice calm, collected and cool.

"I can't, he's moved!" I said, stressed from the strain of waiting to pull the pin on what was obviously a potential muzzleloader world record Shiras moose. "I have to get closer."

And so, for the fourth time, I had to leave a perfect rest and work my way down the hill, following the bull and his smaller buddy as they fed toward cover. No one's ever said taping a TV show is easy. For the previous hour we'd been within range of the moose, but every time we decided to shoot, either Steve or I would call the shot off; the angle was wrong, a tree was in the way, the lighting wasn't right. Long story short, we stalked one last time to within what should have been easy range for my Knight muzzleloader, and I took a rest.

"OK, I'm ready, take him," Steve confirmed.

"I can't, the other bull is standing behind him," I said. There was no choice but to wait again.

That's when I felt the tiny puff of wind on the back of my neck.

"Oh-oh."

The great bull lifted his even greater nose and sucked in several gallons of fresh, mountain air, air now laced with smelly human molecules.

"He's going!" I rose and whispered urgently to Steve. "I gotta' go after him! Tape what you can, but I'm shootin'!"

Poor planning and research doomed the author's first attempt for Shiras moose in Wyoming. The way it turned out, he should have been elk hunting instead.

Ahh, but isn't the line between "hero" and "goat" oh so fine?

I raced forward and pulled up short a breathless nano-second after the moose stopped to see what insignificant creature dared to follow. Broadside he stood, staring at me. In one motion I raised my trusty muzzleloader and fired … too quickly I'm afraid. And that's how a muzzleloader hunter misses a moose that's standing wide open at 66 yards. The giant Shiras moose walked off, unscathed and I, standing there with an empty gun, was forced to face reality on the first morning of my hunt. I'd blown it! Needless to say, I was filled with self-loathing.

Before I could find a bridge to jump off, the sound of "snickering" broke the quiet mountain air. I'd forgotten about the witnesses—my guide, Tory Brock, and, of course, Steve.

"You didn't happen to tape me missing did you?" I asked Steve.

"Oh yeah," he said.

"You aren't still taping right now are you?" I asked.

"Oh yeah," he said.

GETTING THERE

Maybe the miss wouldn't have been so bad if it wasn't for the fact that the hunt had actually started three years before when I decided to apply for a "limited entry" Shiras moose tag. I filled out the various forms, looked at all the hunting options and made my choices, basing my decisions entirely on the "ee-nee-meeny-minny-moe" theory.

A couple months later, what do you know if the mailman didn't bring me a letter from the Wyoming Game Department conceding that I'd drawn a once-in-a-lifetime Shiras moose tag! Never again could I apply to hunt moose in that state, but I didn't care, it had to be a good hunt or else it wouldn't be a once-in-a-lifetime draw. Right?

Picking an outfitter was easy. Wyoming is a big, wild place, but the name Ron Dube just might be bigger and wilder. I remember long ago reading about the "Dube Death March" a reference to Mr. Dube's hunting style. I picked up the phone and with respect, called this living legend.

Ultimate Big Game Adventures

"Yes sir, I do outfit in that area you were drawn for, and you're welcome to stay at my elk camp there. You can pack in on one of my mules ... but I have to tell you that moose are few and far between. Your odds aren't good," Dube said.

Of course, I only heard the "Yes sir" part. He called me sir!

I won't bore you with the messy details, the finagling it took to come up with the mega-dollars it cost for the moose tag and plane ticket to Cody, Wyoming, but suffice-it-to-say, I did. My hero, Jim Zumbo, met me at the airport and delivered me unto my bona fide Wyoming, Ron Dube-supplied mule; but not before he questioned my rationale for applying in such a poor moose area.

"Shockey, you dummy. Why didn't you apply for elk in that zone instead of moose?" Zumbo asked. "Dube's hunters take great elk, but no one in his right mind hunts there for moose."

Of course, I was so awe-struck that the great Dalai Zumbo himself actually met me at the Cody airport, I didn't hear a word he said. And so, after a long flight and eight hours on top of a mule (believe it or not, my Mighty Dodge

No amount of riding and hiking produced hide nor hair of a Shiras moose.

rides smoother), I pulled into Ron Dube's incredible wilderness elk camp. Located outside the far edge of Yellowstone Park, the camp is truly traditional.

Straight to the cook tent I headed.

There, around the long table sat seven elk hunters and their seven guides; talking not about moose, but about elk.

"What'd yours score anyway, 340 or 350?" one asked.

"Three-forty-five, same as the one you got today," the other replied.

"How many bulls did you guys see? Lots?" a guide asked.

"Yeah. You?" a hunter replied.

"Same. Bugling all over the place," the hunter replied.

"Hey guys, name's Shockey, how big are the moose you've been seeing?" I asked.

Silence.

"Bet they're grunting like crazy right?" I

The author's guide, Lonnie Fultz, worked his tail off, but you can't find what isn't there.

tried again.

Silence.

Oh-oh. In the back of my mind there was a little voice saying, "Everyone told you so."

For three days, Ron Dube and my hard-working volunteer moose guide, Lonnie Fultz, did everything but back flips trying to find me a moose. Unfortunately, as I'd been duly warned, the floppy-nosed beasts just plain weren't there. Possibly, I came to realize, because the elk had the place overrun. Each day when we returned to camp, there was another one or two impressive bull elk hanging from the meat pole. While looking for moose I saw bull elk and while listening for moose I heard bull elk; they were everywhere.

Alas, with nary a moose track anywhere in my entire once-in-a-lifetime moose draw zone, I decided to call it a hunt and packed out with the seven hugely successful elk hunters when they left.

TWO YEARS LATER ...

"Yiibbibbbiidddyyibbibbibdddyyyibbbidddde eee ..."

"What's he saying?" I was still holding my hand up as the auctioneer called the going price on the Shiras moose hunt. "Am I winning?"

My wife just shook her head.

"It's for a good cause, Sweetie-pie," I said. "All the money raised here at the Foundation for North American Wild Sheep auction goes toward conservation."

"Yibbidddddidbyddddyiiiiibbiiddddydbiiibb-biddeee ..."

"And it's better to buy a Governor's Shiras moose tag once, than go on 10 expensive hunts and never get a moose! Right?" Convinced, I poked my hand even higher into the air. "I can hunt anywhere in the state, two weeks before the regular season and I can use rifle, muzzle-loader or bow!" I exclaimed, resting my case.

"Going once, going twice ... sold! To the fellow with the wife who isn't going to talk to him for the next two years!" the auctioneer said.

And that's how I came to be looking for a bridge to jump off, watching the giant bull walk away. One second the moose was standing there and the next second, after I fired, he was still standing there in exactly the same different spot! Needless to say, the rest of that first day was uneventful, if not depressing. We saw a few moose, but nothing near the caliber of the moose I'd taken a poke at that morning. Tory had been scouting before the season and had seen many moose, but the one I'd missed was the biggest.

"Think he'll come back to the meadow tomorrow morning?" I asked without really thinking there was much of a chance.

"Might." Tory sounded less than sure.

Less than sure or not, I made up my mind to spend the remainder of the hunt hunting that bull.

After missing a gimme shot at this same huge bull the first day of his hunt, the author redeemed himself on day two.

The second morning of the hunt, we were right back on the big bull's turf. Only he wasn't. We waited until mid-morning before throwing in the towel and heading back to the truck.

"Maybe we should still-hunt back through the timber," Tory suggested.

The going was going to be ugly and loud and with three of us stomping around, there was about a snowball's chance in (you know where) of sneaking up on a wary, old, and once-shot-at, bull moose.

"Tory!" I grabbed my guide and aimed his body to the side. "Moose!"

We'd been walking for about 15 minutes when I'd happened to look to the side and noticed the long, black nose and one beady eye staring at us through the trees.

"It's him!" Tory picked the bull up in the binos and confirmed that, indeed, the bull standing 30 yards away was the giant bull that I'd missed the day before.

The shot wasn't my favorite, the bull wasn't broadside, but when the cap popped on my .50 caliber Knight muzzleloader, I was sure that the bullet had flown true. The bull heaved from sight in an instant.

We found the giant bull a short distance away and only then began to realize just how big he really was. His antlers were more than 53 inches wide, very unusual for a Shiras, and it was pretty obvious that he'd be a world record muzzleloader moose. That fact was confirmed officially after the velvet was stripped off, and the bull was scored several months later. I still shudder when I think that I missed this same bull standing broadside at 66 yards. When skill fails, it's nice to know that fate and luck are sometimes there to pick up the slack! ■

CHAPTER TWENTY:
VALLEY OF THE MOOSE

One, two, three … eight, nine … thirteen, fourteen. Another bull moose stood up in the mountain alder patch half-a-mile away.

"Fourteen moose in a 2-acre patch!" The sight was so impressive that I just had to vent my excitement to my hunting partner." Seven bulls and seven cows! That makes more than 30 moose sightings today!"

"We're hunting elk," he replied.

My hunting partner knew me well enough to know that if he didn't keep me focused on elk, a moose hunting I would go.

"You know the season's open," I said, grudgingly returning to elk glassing. And I have a moose tag."

Now, there are those who would crawl a mile across broken glass just to hear an elk bugle, but I'm not one of them. Don't get me wrong. During the elk rut, in the early morn, when the sky reddens and the sun is still an hour below the horizon, there is nothing like the sound of an elk bugle reverberating among the silhouetted mountain peaks. It's like attending the symphony. In the dark before the show, the orchestra tunes, and the crowd whispers. Then slowly, one by one, the voices still and for a few moments before the performance, the theater is deathly still.

It happens in the mountains, too. The world hushes, and the first bull elk of the day wets his ivories; mellifluous, he whistles through the scale. Another answers, then another—a veritable chorus. A symphony. Pretty, like the elk itself. The elk … prince of the forest.

What can I say, I'm not a symphony fan or an elk kinda' guy. Give me the backbeat of a rock concert any day. Raw and powerful. Big and tough like the moose. When the moose rut is in full swing, the audience doesn't need decorum and it mustn't quiet down. The call of the cow moose alone will overpower the forest.

When a cow moose points her big hairy nose heavenward and belches out her passion, there is no denying the depth of her desire.

135

No tuned and structured musical scale for her. The cow moose, plain and simple, lets it all hang out.

EEEowwwEEE000000000hhhhhhhaaaahhh-hugfff! There's no accounting for taste, and I grant you that a bull elk bugle is inspirational. But for pure energy, there is nothing as beautiful, in a "gimme' lovin' right now" kind of way, as a cow moose moaning somewhere out in the fog of a muskeg swamp.

The bull moose call is different. A bull moose call is understated, not the prima donna performance of a bull elk. The bull moose call lacks the bravado of the bull elk. The bull moose is a hulking thug looking for a fight. He's not trying to sound tough, he is tough. He's not trying to sound handsome, pretty or princely. He's none of these, he knows.

UUUGGMMFF! He's not bluffing. UUUG-GMFF! He's coming and intends to have his way.

The hunter desiring adventure needn't look further than the moose rut. Imitate the yearning yodel of the cow moose on an early October morn if you dare. But understand that when the bull moose comes to you, he's looking for one of two things—lovin' or a fight. And more than likely, when he finds an imposter standing in the spot where he expected to find a lovely, hairy-nosed, kitten d'amour, he's going to forget kissin' and start stompin.'

They won't find your body until the next time the bull cleans between his toenails!

"Ahem?!" My hunting partner was shaking the daydreams out of me. "I've been trying to get your attention for the last five minutes! Where the heck have you been? Disneyland?"

"I'm coming back," I said, my mind made up. "I'm coming back during the rut! I've never seen a valley with so many moose. I'm coming back!"

My partner shook his head.

"Fine. You can chase swamp donkeys next month, but right now try and think elk," he said, shaking his head in disgust. "I know how hard it is for you to think at all, let alone think

Unlike his Shiras moose hunting adventures, this time the author found moose on his elk hunt in British Columbia. Returning a year later, he kept dreaming of the place he had dubbed "valley of the moose."

about something classy like an elk, but try."

As soon as he finished, I was back to day-dreaming about moose.

MOOSE ESSENTIALS

The Canada moose, like those in the valley, is the middle-sized member of the moose family. It's also the most widely distributed. I was hunting in British Columbia, north of where the Shiras moose is found, and south of where the massive Alaska-Yukon moose resides.

Of course, the term massive is relative. A full-grown Canada moose will still tip the scales at nearly 1,200 pounds and stand 7 feet at the shoulder. The antlers of an exceptional bull will spread out 5 feet tip to tip and sport more than 10 points a side. With statistics like these, you can quickly understand why I wax poetic about the mammoth beasts.

Moose, like all the other members of the deer family, have excellent vision and olfactory senses—even better than the white-tailed deer, some

believe. I can't say for sure whether they have better noses than whitetails, but they certainly have bigger noses. They have bigger ears as well and, again, because of this, there are those moose lovers who think that the moose has better hearing than a deer. There is only one department where moose aficionados grant the whitetail a point, and that's in the looks department. Moose are a lot of things, but pretty ain't one of them.

RETURN ENGAGEMENT

The moose that I saw during my elk hunt were high in the alpine, above the late-summer flies. When they lay down in the willowy brush patches, they disappeared. But when they stood, they stood out like big, black sore thumbs on the mountainsides.

Exactly one month to the day, I was back in the valley of the moose. Instead of the green rolling alpine, I found a valley awash in a kaleidoscope sea of red, yellow and orange. The air was far fresher than the muggy heat of August,

It's rare to have a problem with too many moose, but it happened during this adventure as the author tried to approach the herd bull.

and, I quickly learned, the moose were moving.

This time, I had a video cameraman along and a young wrangler to look after the horses. We'd arrived in the valley the day before, but waited for the following morning to saddle up and head to the back end where I'd seen the moose. Two hours into the trip, before we were halfway up the valley, we spied our first bull, a decent 45-incher. Nice and, at 15 yards, big, but not the bull I was hoping to find. My plan was to head up the valley, make camp and spend several days looking for a honking big bull — one that would supply my family with several hundred pounds of moose burger and chewy steaks and would qualify among the top five in the muzzleloader record book.

We had just reached the back end of the valley, and hadn't even unpacked the horses when I noticed eight moose in a swamp, half a mile away. One was a paddle-horned brute and so,

before you can say, "stop and think about it," we were trotting mooseward.

"Sssstt," The wrangler was tugging at my jacket and pointing over my shoulder.

"What?" My tone made it clear that I wasn't impressed, at least not until I looked where he was pointing. "Oh."

There, standing directly in the path that we'd decided to take to the big bull, was another big bull. This one was wider, but didn't have as many points. The one we wanted had 15 points per side including two nontypical points sticking out the back of one paddle.

"Too small," I said, shaking my head knowing there was no such thing as a small moose. "We'll have to cut down lower."

Fifty yards later, still several hundred yards from the big bull and his harem, I felt my jacket being tugged again.

"Bull," was all the wrangler said.

Ultimate Big Game Adventures

Preoccupied with the rut, this bull waited too long to exit stage right.

Another bull, smaller, stepped from a 10-foot-tall mountain alder patch. Again we worked our way lower, past this inquisitive bull.

"Oh-oh." This time it was my cameraman who spoke. "I think we're surrounded."

Two more bulls appeared, one on each side of us. The other two were following.

"Don't anybody make a moose call," I joked … kind of.

By then, there was really nowhere to go but straight ahead, damn the torpedoes; we had to get to within 100 yards of the biggest bull, close enough for a shot with my Knight muzzleloader. Fortunately, the satellite bulls all around us by then were rut-crazed enough to watch rather than run. Or maybe they knew our intentions.

Finally, nearly an hour after we first spotted the bull, we were in position; the camera rolled and the final act began. The bull stared up at us

and our antlered buddies, obviously unhappy. His neck swelled and he stood to his full height in the waist-deep alders. To this day, I wonder what would have happened if one of us would have cow-called. At the time, surrounded by all those rutting bull moose, I would have bet that all three of us would have ended up trampled.

BOOOMMM!

The decision was easy. The bull started walking, obviously headed in a direction that would cut our scent. The instant that he cleared the last cow, I gently squeezed the trigger, sending the bullet on its way.

As the bull tipped over, I made another promise to myself, the same one that I'd made the month before during my elk hunt. I'm coming back.

Author's note: The bull's antlers measured 53 inches. He placed fifth in the muzzleloader record book and he was definitely chewy. ∎

Chapter Twenty: Valley Of the Moose

CHAPTER TWENTY-ONE:

BULLS AND BILLIES

shivered. Sitting alone under a tree on a remote mountain all night isn't so bad. Or at least it isn't when you've just spent a month backpacking around the mountains of British Columbia. You toughen up. Besides, I had anticipation to keep me warm; there was a giant bull moose out in the darkness, somewhere close. I'd seen the bull with his harem of three cows two days before. He shouldn't have gone far, and, with a bit of luck, I'd see him come morning. I shivered again.

When I'd first seen him I'd opted to leave him be. Partly my decision had to do with the fact that my hunting partner and I were out of supplies. We needed to head back out of the mountains to our camper. We needed to replenish our supplies and restock our dwindling resolve. A month in the mountains might toughen your body, but the constant vigilance, inadequate caloric intake and demanding climate play havoc on your desire.

We'd returned to the camper, eaten a real meal and slept in almost-real beds. Our decision to return to the relative security of our camper proved fortuitous. During the night a storm struck, rocking the camper and depositing several inches of fresh snow.

MOOSE!

Never before have I seen such a sight. From our camper, we could see a dozen bull moose on the mountainsides around us. Where they'd been almost impossible to pick out the day before, they now appeared like blatant black bull's eyes. As the bulls walked across the mountainsides, they knocked the snow from the waist-high buck brush, leaving a ribbon of snow-less foliage in their wake, much like the trail a jet leaves in the sky.

To that point in the hunt, we'd been reluctant to take a moose, even though we both had moose tags and had seen dozens of bulls. Our reasoning was sound. If we killed a moose, the hunt would be, for all intents and purposes, over. Once you have one moose on the ground, you often have days of work ahead of you and need to get the meat cooled quickly. Since we were in an area as remote as you can get to by vehicle, we'd chosen to concentrate on mountain goats for the first weeks of our trip. Now the end of the hunt was nigh, and it was time to get serious about finding a couple suitable moose.

TIME TO STRIKE

My partner hadn't killed a moose before, so when we spied one that we figured would make for a full freezer, there was no holding

him back. Almost before I had a chance to wish him luck, he had his backpack on and was headed up the mountain. I remained picky. My determination was fire-tempered with the knowledge that one of the moose that I'd turned down earlier in the hunt turned out to be a huge 59-inch, 30-point bull that another hunter harvested the day after I turned it down.

By lunchtime the snow had melted, and the easy moose spotting was history. About then, my partner strolled in wearing a smile as wide as the antlers he carried on his back. Why he wore such a big smile I'll never know, but I do know that it wasn't nearly as big the next day after the 10th backpack trip up the mountain for the meat. I've hauled my share of moose out of the mountains before, so I never had a smile to begin with.

By the time that we had the meat hauled in, the thought of the big moose that we'd spotted two days before haunted me. How big was it exactly? As soon as we hauled the last load of meat into camp, I loaded up my backpack and headed back up the river drainage. It would be a solo hunt; my partner had to take care of 600 or so pounds of moose meat.

I was on a mission. When I reached where we'd set up a spike camp the week before, I dropped my gear and headed deeper into the wilds carrying nothing but my survival pack and Knight muzzleloader. I intended to cut the distance and try to re-spot the bull, judge him and then determine how best to stalk him the next day.

I set up and glassed from the first ridge with no result. Then the second and the third. Eventually by about the fifth ridge I had to make a decision; should I go on? If I did I'd be spending the night under a tree. Or should I head back to base camp? I chose to go on, but as it turned out, I never found the bull that evening.

When morning came, it did so sluggishly. "With child" clouds hung heavy over the mountaintops, promising snow. The bull hadn't been there the evening before when I tucked myself under my tree, but now he was standing

Moose in the valleys, goats on the mountains. It's one of Canada's great combos.

Ultimate Big Game Adventures

Look before you leap. These are words that mountain goat hunters live by. Without a safe route to approach within range and a safe place for the goat to fall, you're wasting time and energy.

with his harem a mere 800 yards away. Checking my Knight muzzleloader automatically, I was stalking up the mountain within minutes.

All looked good until I slid over the last ridge. I'd been out of sight of the bull for the hour that it had taken me to make the stalk, and he was gone! I crawled higher on the ridge, in full sight, hoping to find some clue.

That's when the first cow rose from her bed. She made me immediately and, after deciding that I was trouble, she woofed loudly, turned hoof and fled. Two other cows followed. About that instant I saw the tip of an antler down in the buck brush just below where I waited ... and

waited. It seemed an eternity, a standoff. While
I waited for the bull to make his move, I had
time to reflect on the beginning of our hunt.

GOATS FIRST

For as far back as I can remember, my father
and I talked about hunting mountain goats.
Back then, living on the bald prairies, it was
nothing but talk, a dream. Then with my move
to the coast for university, the dream became
more than talk. It became several seasons' worth
of lung-searing, muscle-tearing, real-life ordeals.

As I waited for the bull to rise from his bed, I
recalled all the mountains that my partner and I
had climbed during the previous few weeks.
Always, after pounding our way to the top,
we'd find the goats were too far, too high or too
something to go after. It wasn't until the third
week of the hunt that we finally found goats in
a huntable spot.

The day before we found them, we'd climbed
for hours to make it to a high alpine valley. That
night, by the light of the northern lights we
slurped in a meal of the finest freeze-dried food,
nursed blisters and eventually slept like rocks,
on rocks. We awoke to a grey world of fog.
With nothing better to do, we settled in with a
mug of coffee and waited. It's beautiful actually.
Sitting in the fog, I mean. Sounds are muted,
and the world around you presses in. There
isn't much to say, nor is there any reason to say
much. Each of us was lost in our own thoughts.

In a way I would have preferred to keep it like

*While the author's cousin, Guy, enjoyed moose
on a stick, the author spent a cold night under
a tree hoping for a moose of his own.*

that for a while longer, but it didn't happen.
Around noon that day, the sun broke through
the fog, illuminating three billies on a rock face
a mile away. I stalked them and closed the distance to 200 yards before running out of cover. I
tried to use a passing bit of fog to hide my
advance, but was caught in the open when the
fog suddenly lifted. The billy goats made me
and climbed into some cliffs that I'd have needed a catapult to reach.

Within the hour I was back at camp. That's
when we noticed a goat almost straight above
us. It was making its way carefully along a
rocky ledge and looked to be a huge, old, yel-
low-hued billy. Again the hunt was going to be
a tough one. And once again I missed my
chance. My hunting partner watched the
whole affair from far below. As I slipped up
one side of a ridge; the billy walked by me on
the other side. At one point we were only 50
yards apart.

By the time I returned to camp for the second
time in the day, I was exhausted and more than
willing to call it quits. I'd just settled in when
we noticed another big billy standing in the
rocks on the far side of the valley! Inspired, I
picked up my muzzleloader and trotted toward
the billy. At least I trotted the downhill part. On
the far side of the valley, my trot slowed to a

A week after taking a mountain goat, the author's persistence paid off with this great British Columbia bull.

grunting, lurching walk.

Before the hour was out, I'd worked my way to within 130 yards of the old goat. Even at that distance I could tell that he was a giant. With a rifle the shot was a gimme, but with my muzzleloader, at the angle the goat rested, I had no shot. I waited one very long, cold hour. It started to rain, and the wind picked up. I wore only a shirt on my upper body and plastered as I was against a rock face, it offered little protection and less comfort.

Who knows why the billy finally decided to stand? Certainly it wasn't because he was growing concerned for my advancing hypothermia; more likely the approaching dusk dictated his movement. Whatever the reason, he stood, and I squeezed the trigger.

Even as I waited for the bull moose to rise now a week later, I felt a tinge of remorse. A famous philosopher once wrote, "I do not hunt to kill, I kill to have hunted." Every hunter knows well what he meant. Hunting is the condition of desiring the condition of desire, not the desire of the object of desire.

The barest hint of movement from below brought me back to the moment, the hunt. The bull that I'd been waiting for was about to get up! His nerve finally broke and he heaved to his feet to see what had frightened his cows away. When he did, I placed the crosshairs low behind his front shoulder.

The huge beast stood magnificent in the tangled mountain alder. His legs were black and back golden, bleached by the sun. Maybe he knew his time was up, maybe not. Maybe he, like I, knew that we were both acting out our parts in Nature's drama.

I hoped so. ∎

CHAPTER TWENTY-TWO:

HUNTING THE DEVIL'S BATH

No fly has been trussed more surly, caught in a spider's web.

So was I caught by the silence, listening. What was the other-worldly sound that had torn me from slumber? My arms were pinned in my sleeping bag. Every nerve ending crackled. I wanted to move, wanted to free my arms and reach for my firearm, do something proactive to defend myself. But against what?

Instinct demanded flight or fight, but I could do neither until I identified the sound. In those minutes of waiting I cursed the technology that produced the nylon covering my sleeping bag. The wonder material rustled loudly at the barest movement, I dared not try to free my arms lest I provoke whatever was outside the flimsy wall of the backpack tent.

As the minutes passed in deathly silence, my heartbeat slowed. Perhaps I'd been mistaken; maybe it was a dream, a horrible one. Maybe it was nothing. I was fading back to sleep when the sound ripped through the pitch-black stillness for the second time.

This time I reacted. Before the sound faded, my arms were free and I was sitting up with my rifle in hand. The sound was unlike anything that I'd experienced in my many years of wilderness hunting and camping. Not exactly a moan and not exactly a scream, it was more of an insane shriek.

Then I heard it breathe.

UNFORGIVING AND HARSH

There is no such thing as a mundane mountain goat hunt. There can't be. The very nature of the beast inspires descriptions like "visceral," "breathtaking" and "dicey." The simple truth is, mountain goats live where humans cannot, should not and for that matter, would not, want to live. Humans, pathetic creatures that we are, aren't designed to survive for long in the inhospitable climes favored by even the meekest mountain goat.

They live where cragged points and ridges heave from near vertical mountainsides; where pinnacles and boulders poke and hang impossible, above and beyond the reach of physical law. They live where grey shale faces shape-shift into slides, innocuous, a trap for the unwary and where glaciers have cleaved and calved for 10,000 years. It is in these places that the mountain goats live; in the rocky turmoil of the high peaks, unforgiving and harsh. A devil's bath of roiling granite. And it is here that the hunter must willingly and with determination

A mountain goat hunt is a journey; first by boat or plane or horse, then, inevitably, frighteningly sometimes, by foot. Mountain goats live in some of God's most glorious places, but places better suited to goat feet than human feet. Danger and the devil lurk.

go, if, that is, the hunter wishes to gaze upon these magnificent, wild creatures.

Unfortunately, for the weekend warrior, there is no easy way to get to where the mountain goats reside. Fortunately, for the serious hunter, there is no easy way to get to where the mountain goats reside. Perfection. Absolute solitude awaits. Virtually no one, other than serious hunters, purposely seeks out mountain goats outside the boundaries of the manicured "wilderness-like" parks. Never have the words, "Be the honor equal to the task," (obviously spoken by some goatward-bound hunter), rang more true. The task of "getting there" is often as adventure-filled as the hunt itself.

GETTING THERE

I've used planes, trucks, boats, horses and boots to get into goat country, with mixed results, at least as far as bringing back a goat goes, but always with success in the adventure department. During my last attempt to hunt goats, I had myself flown into a remote mountain lake along the coast. Actually, a remote mountain lake surrounded by jagged, Cessna-munching mountains might better describe the insignificant blue drip of water that I looked down upon from 5,000 feet.

"You mean that's the lake I wanted you to land on?" I yelled above the engine noise.

"Yep," the pilot said, flaring the tiny plane into a deep, banking dive.

"Hey! I have a way better idea!" I grabbed the pilot's shoulder and pointed. "How about let's

land over there on that big lake!"

"That's the ocean," he said, levelling out and dropping his flaps. "Hang on."

We were headed directly toward a tiny V-crack in the cliffs.

To the best of my recollection, I said something to the effect of "AAAAEEEEEEEEEE!"

Suffice it to say, taking off from the lake was even more of an adventure.

On another mountain goat hunt, one detailed later in this book, while hiking up the mountain in a snowstorm, I fell into a freezing river right at dark. Only by the good grace of Providence did I manage to find an abandoned outfitter's cabin and save myself. My rifle stock was broken and my scope mangled, but after an evening of intensive care, the mess of steel and wood was at least functional. I had to stalk to within 20 yards of the mountain goat to be sure of placing a bullet humanely, but all ended well.

On at least two mountain goat hunts, grizzly bear encounters on the trail leading up to goat country overshadowed the excitement of the actual goat hunt. It's an expected part of hunting the devil's bath. The devil's own spawn — grizzly bears and the like — guard the way; evil-tempered creatures from the dark recesses they are, creatures that do not tolerate intrusion by mere mortals.

MOUNTAIN GOAT ESSENTIALS

Nasty as mountain goat country is, there isn't really a "best" time to hunt for these special animals. Instead there are "less worse" times. No

matter when the hunter chooses to brave the dangers of a mountain goat hunt, the devil's bath is never welcoming. That said, early hunts, those that take place during August, are the easiest in terms of weather. These same hunts, however, do not produce the best mountain goats as they're still sporting their sparse summer coats.

Compared to a mountain sheep, a mountain goat is "horn-ally challenged," but what it doesn't have sticking out of its head, it more then makes up for in hide and hair. A mature billy, resplendent in his coat of white, would make a Tibetan Yeti jealous. And the best coats, as one might expect, are found on mountain goats near the end of the hunting season, the coldest and nastiest time to be hunting the devil's bath. At this time of year, usually mid-October, a billy goat's "chaps" will hang down well below his knees.

Care must be taken at all times after a hunter enters the devil's bath, but the later in the season, the more it be at the forefront of the hunter's mind. One misstep on an icy slope and it's toboggan time. Imagine "swooshing" off of a 3,000-foot ski jump. Now imagine hitting a rock wall at terminal velocity. Splat. Get the point? Most mountain goat hunters are intelligent enough to stay away from the mountain goat mountains once the snow falls.

Typically, no matter when a hunter chooses to

Sure, you can make it. Glacial rivers and more are likely to stand between you and a mountain goat.

Chapter Twenty-Two: Hunting The Devil's Bath

hunt them, mountain goats must be spotted and then stalked. The former is usually easy, while the latter is always difficult. Seeing a big billy standing wide open on a cliff does not a billy goat rug on the wall make; it takes luck, planning and a bucket of sweat. Somehow the hunter has to make his way above and behind the mountain goat. Neither is easy, especially since behind a goat there is usually a rock face and above is usually nothing but thin air.

Should the hunter manage to pick his way into shooting position, taking the shot depends much more on what will happen to the goat should it be hit. Invariably, if it hasn't been anchored where it stood, it will leap out into space to get away. Again, imagine that 3,000-foot ski jump. While the meat might be tender, the hide and horns will be ruined. For this reason, mountain goat hunters must wait for a shot that will ensure that they recover the goat intact.

CUE THE DEVIL

All this I knew as I waited. Not that it mattered when there was a "thing" waiting out in the darkness. I could hear it suck in air and then exhale in a long, drawn-out, guttural, rasping rattle. It sounded like the devil himself was devouring the souls of the dead. Sitting there, fingers clenched tightly against the cold wood of my rifle stock, it crossed my mind that perhaps it had finally happened and I'd died on the way to the devil's bath, and my present situation was my just reward. Huh! Imagine that! Sure didn't sound like I'd ended up in heaven.

As the dawn greyed, the breathing drifted from my hearing. Eventually I unzipped the tent and looked out into cloud. During the night the cloud cover had settled lower than the tree-line where I was camped. It was so thick that I couldn't see 10 feet into the mist. It was disconcerting, especially so when another banshee shriek pierced the fog. Then another, this one from farther back in the fog on the other side of camp.

However, with the morning came the ability to act, so I broke camp. It was time to run away.

Fog, too, is fairly common in mountain goat climes. When it comes, it is time to wait.

Ultimate Big Game Adventures

Tough to get to, tough to judge, tough to kill. A successful mountain goat hunt is tough to beat.

From what, to be honest, I could not say, but now there were two of the things somewhere out there in the gauze, and it was time for a strategic withdrawal. Mountain goat hunting had never held less appeal than it did right then, there would be other years … maybe.

Whatever they were, they followed me for several hundred yards down the mountainside to the point where I cleared the bottom edge of the clouds. They were always out of sight, but always there, as surely as I was. When I finally broke free of the mist, the creatures let go their hold. It was as if they had never been. The mountain was suddenly just that, a mountain and not a foul place of ghouls and devil spawn.

To this day I don't know what it was. Maybe it was a bear, but I doubt it. They should have been in hibernation by then. A cougar? Could be, but doubtful as far north as that. A wolf then? Possibly, but if it was, it made a sound like no wolf I've ever met. Werewolf maybe, but not a timber wolf. No, if I had to make a guess at it I'd say it must have been a wolverine. "Carcajou." One of the guardians of the gate to the devil's bath. ■

CHAPTER TWENTY-THREE:
CLIMBING SOLO

Every mountain goat hunt is an adventure, and every mountain goat is a trophy.

Somewhere ahead of me a cabin awaited. Behind me loomed an honest six-hour, mostly uphill hike. Above me another foot of snow began to fall, while below a swollen creek roared. Darkness lurked around the corner.

I'd forded the creek once before during the climb up and wasn't thrilled about crossing it again. The first time I'd narrowly averted disaster by making a frantic leap at the far shore as I lost my footing on the icy log spanning the creek. This time I chose a bridge more deliberately.

Balancing on the rock mid-stream, I realized one fundamental flaw in my reckoning. The freezing temperature at this altitude had turned the moisture on each rock into glare ice. I gingerly reached forward placing the butt of my rifle on a rock just under the surface. By holding the barrel near the muzzle, my .300 Weatherby Mark V acted nicely as a third point of support. I shifted my weight to make the long step to the next rock.

Then, in a nightmare come true, the wooden stock snapped at the pistol grip. Leaning on it as I was, I didn't have a chance. One instant I was stepping forward, the next I was laying in the icy water. Even as the current yanked my legs downstream, I wrapped my free arm around a rock and snapped my feet up under me. Quicker than it takes to tell it, I was on the far bank, shaking.

The rifle barrel was still in my hand, and as I climbed out of the stream I remember the sickening sound of what was left of my rifle stock dragging across the rocks. Still attached to the shoulder strap, the piece of fiddleback walnut followed me like a guilty dog.

LIFE OR DEATH DECISION

Worse by far than the ruined rifle, I was now in serious trouble. I had a choice to make and minutes in which to make it. I could stop right where I was and in the fleeting daylight attempt to build a fire. Or I could spend those precious minutes looking for the cabin. I knew that it was supposed to be near the second crossing along the horse trail that I'd been following, but, then again, that information came from the fellow who built the cabin. He'd climb up a mountain and back down just for a look-see, a stroll.

Knowing the cabin to be outfitted with a wood heater, I made my choice. Ice crystals formed on

152

my pants by the time I traveled 200 yards. At a quarter-mile, I was second-guessing myself. The trail, now covered in a blanket of snow, evaporated in the fading light. Then I stumbled into an opening and the cabin.

Numbed, I burst through the low door and struggled to free my pack. Like a shaking drunk, I dropped to my knees and clawed at the heater handle. Paper and kindling waited, all I had to do was strike one of the matches lying on the split board table. Simple. But only after a dozen attempts did I finally manage the faculty to pick up a match, strike it and hold it to the paper. Within minutes the fire roared, forcing the cold from the tiny cabin and my frozen bones.

I was going to live. My rifle was broken in two. My scope was mangled. Best of all, my solo goat hunt was just beginning.

MOUNTAIN GOAT GUTS

British Columbia is the best place in the world to hunt mountain goats; a glance through the record books will confirm this fact. The beautiful creatures can be found almost anywhere in the province, but unless you have good optics or a great pair of legs and lungs, you might never see one.

Interestingly, many hunters don't rate mountain goats highly as a trophy. Too easy to see, the critics say, and once you climb above them you can walk right down on them. Mountain goats never look up for danger, so goes the argument. Uh-huh. Why should they? The only thing above a big billy is usually cliff and thin air, neither of which the most ardent critic of the mountain goat can walk on.

My bet is that most of those same critics don't have a mountain goat on their wall, let alone a big, old billy. Therein lies another problem with goat hunting, that being exactly how difficult it is to tell a big, old billy from any other goat. They are one of the most difficult big game animals to field judge. Even with the best optics in the world, an 8-inch billy—an OK goat—is almost impossible to differentiate from a 9-inch billy—a good goat. A 10-inch billy is a whopper. On the other hand, a 10-inch nanny is not uncommon. When looking from a distance, the only real way to tell a lone billy from a lone nanny is horn circumference. To complicate matters, you are normally doing all this judging from a couple miles

away on another mountain; guaranteed to be one deep valley and one raging creek away.

Oh sure, you can walk over to take a closer look, but can and do were never so distant. You have to be three-quarters mountain man and one-quarter Loony Tunes to stalk closer to every goat you see, just to be better able to field judge it. Unfortunately, while most of us hunters qualify in the Loony Tunes department, we fall a little shy as mountain men. Three-quarters accountant just doesn't cut the mustard in the mountains.

NO LOOKING BACK

I proved myself in the Loony Tunes department right at the outset of my hunt. The weather was downright ornery. It took 4-wheel-drive to coax my truck the last 20 miles up the logging road that took me to the trailhead. The snow was 6 inches deep and still falling where I parked and got deeper the higher I climbed. Sadly, I didn't have anyone to complain to because I was hunting solo; partially by choice and partially because I couldn't find anyone else as dumb.

Shouldering my heavy pack, I'd taken one last look at my truck before heading up the horse trail for my planned one-week hunt. Fifty yards later I took another look back and reconsidered. I stood in a grizzly bear track so fresh that the falling snow hadn't blemished the smoking-hot, foot-long tracks. The bear was headed up the same horse trail that I had to take.

For the first hour I climbed fully expecting to bump into the big bruin, but he proved a capable climber and eventually veered off the trail. During the next several hours I climbed through cloud. Only once did the cloud lift long enough for me to glimpse the mountainside on the opposite side of the valley. My spirits soared at the sight of three goats sleeping on a rock bluff half-a-mile away. How could I help but be optimistic?

Sitting at the table in the cabin, looking at the mess that used to be a fine rifle, however, all optimism shattered. My hunt appeared over. The thought of climbing down the next day, driving 14 hours home, picking out another rifle and repeating the whole process, lacked appeal.

Desperate, I pulled out the roll of emergency packing tape that I always carry in my pack. I borrowed a butter knife from the cabin cutlery jar and began wrapping. Half-an-hour later my rifle

It's no wonder that the author took this photo of this cabin. The shelter probably saved his life on his solo goat adventure.

was splinted and taped into some semblance of its original self. I couldn't remove the scope, but discovered that if I turned the rifle sideways and looked down the rifle barrel, lining up on the right angle where the forestock met the barrel, I'd have a rudimentary sight. A few minutes with my backpacking saw, and the bothersome comb was gone. I was back in business.

FOGGY CHANCES

The next morning I woke to the same cloudy, zero-visibility weather. After several hours of futile wandering, I returned to the cabin to dry out. The next day, same thing.

At dusk the third day, I got my first break. The clouds lifted long enough for a quick look at the surrounding mountains. In moments I spied five yellow-looking rocks high on a slope. Goats! But before I could set up my spotting scope, the clouds returned.

Day four began exactly as the three previous days but was, if anything, colder. I waited for an hour hoping for better visibility, but it was not to be. Time to gamble. I believed that the goats would be close to where I'd seen them the day before and reasoned that my only hope was to climb blind and hope that I bumped into them. If I found them in the gloom, they would be close. Which is just what I needed with my jerry-rigged rifle.

Three hours of miserable climbing through 2 feet of snow brought me to a ridgetop. Peeking over, I saw goats! One nanny and kid fed just 30

yards away, and another nanny and kid were bedded beyond. I ducked back behind the protection of the ridge and made my way another 100 yards up the slope.

I peeked again. Another nanny and kid. The nanny was truly a trophy. Her long, hooked horns curled up and back nearly 12 inches above her forehead. If not for the kid, I would have shot her.

Then at 40 yards, the back of a third goat appeared. As the rest of the goat materialized, I judged it as a young billy. The goat was far from a record-book contender, but, under the circumstances, everything I could have hoped for. When the goat closed to within 30 yards, I gently squeezed the trigger.

That mountain goat hangs on my wall now, a constant reminder of something that many hunters do not realize. Every mountain goat hunt is an adventure, and every mountain goat is a trophy. ∎

CHAPTER TWENTY-FOUR:

UP & DOWN MOUNTAIN GOATS

"Mountain goat hunting" isn't in the dictionary, but if it were, the definition would simply read ... "up and down." Nothing more, nothing less.

While I waited for the verdict, I gazed in awe over the far side of the ridge. There, 1,000 feet below, a massive glacier swept away, coursing through a dozen miles of solid granite. At first glance it looked to be flowing. At longer glance, say a 10,000-year-long glance, one would see that it was flowing; a veritable river of ice, hundreds of feet deep, grinding its way toward the distant ocean. ...

"There he is!" said my hunting partner for the day, Bryan Martin, as he slid down the smooth boulder and faced me. "He's the one we're after!"

It had taken us four hours to climb to where we could see the awesome ice flow, but at Bryan's words, the glacier suddenly held all the allure of an ice cube. Forgetting the view below, I turned to wriggle my way up the boulder for a peek. The big goat didn't stand out like a blast of pure white among the grey strewn boulders breaking the ridge-line, and it took me a moment to locate him. When I did, though, I was caught up in the hunt more surely than any fly was ever caught in a spider's web. He was beautiful, bedded and, best of all, approachable!

The "up" part of mountain goat hunting never gets more "up" than when the hunter first spies a magnificent and huntable billy. Usually these great beasts will stand aloof in the windswept peaks, just as obvious as they are impossibly inaccessible, a vertical mile above where the wishful goat hunter watches through a spotting scope. Speaking both literally and figuratively, getting close to a full-grown billy goat is the highest of all hunting's many highs.

WATCH YOUR STEP

It took Bryan and me two more hours to work our way along the rugged northern facing glacier side of the ridge. We didn't rest until we figured that we were within muzzleloader dis-

tance of the big goat. We could have made it quicker, but several times we turned back to seek out a safer route through the cliffs and rock bluffs guarding the glacial birthing grounds. Oh sure, we probably could have navigated some of the uglier cracks and crevices, the ones that disappeared like icy veins into the cold heart of the glacier, but neither one of us wanted to end up as specimens on some archaeologist's dissecting table.

"And so, my esteemed colleagues, we leave the frozen mastodon exhibit and present you with these two 21st century mountain goat hunters we found frozen in a glacier. Please ignore the 'Dumb' and 'Dumber' name tags we've attached to their toes, just a little laboratory humor, and instead notice how one of these ancient primitives was hunting with a muzzleloader!"

You get the point. Crevices were out; discretion was in.

Once we were in place, tucked behind a rock outcropping, I went through the checklist to make sure that my Knight muzzleloader was ready to perform; preparing for what we hoped was the dying act of the play. Bryan motioned for me to take the first look, which, when I was ready, I did.

Big mistake.

Unfortunately, somehow during the stalk I'd lost my bearings and thought that the goat was in one spot when, in fact, he was in another. Instead of me spying the billy first, the goat and I locked eyes at the same instant. Both of us instantly reacted to that "oh-oh" feeling the same way; we started scrambling! Me to raise my muzzleloader, and the goat to vacate that part of the mountain. The goat was quicker.

"We can still go after him," Bryan said, watching the spooked goat through his spotting scope. "He's not looking back anymore. He's going to bed right there on the edge of that drop-off."

In the 40 minutes that had passed since I'd blown the stalk, the sting of defeat wasn't fading. If anything was fading it was my desire to continue the hunt. It was my last day, and this was the second billy during the three-day hunt that had been within shooting range. The first walked directly below my hunting partner,

Gregg Gutschow, and I, only 80 yards away, but I'd elected to let that goat keep walking. I was leaning over a shelf, literally aiming straight down and didn't have a clue where to hold on a target that was located at six o'clock.

The "down" part of mountain goat hunting is never more "down" than when you've worked your tail off, stalked to within spitting distance of a billy goat and then let the shot clock run out.

KEEP CLIMBING

"Look, we can sneak all the way up this ridge, down the back of that one and we'll pop up 30 yards from where he's standing," Bryan said, offering encouragement and optimism.

I looked before daring to hope. Bryan was right, we could do all of that, but even if we got close enough to take a shot, the goat might bail over the edge of the drop-off and fall 3,000 feet into the lake that we'd walked up from that morning. If he did, there'd only be a goaty-looking oil slick on the lake surface to tell of the bad shot that I'd chosen to take. Besides, even if the goat didn't go over the edge, by the time we finished stalking, shooting and skinning him, we wouldn't be starting our walk back down the mountain until it was nearly dark!

I thought for a moment more. "OK," I said.

The fastest way to a goat is rarely a straight line, nor is it usually the safest way.

Ultimate Big Game Adventures

"Let's give it another try."

My logic in deciding to go after the goat wasn't without fault, I admit, and wisdom was admittedly lacking, but when there is a 10-inch billy in the spotting scope, logic and wisdom must be tempered with a little hope that someone might answer a prayer. And so, before you can say, "Gosh, it's taken three hours, that goat is a lot farther away than we thought" or "Maybe we should have reconsidered the ramifications of climbing off the mountain in the dark," Bryan and I were edging our way along the top edge of the drop-off.

If we had any luck going our way, it was that the goat appeared to be bedded on a ledge that we hadn't seen from our original vantage, and if I could anchor him in place ... he just might not kick over the drop-off.

"Ready?" I mouthed to Bryan. He gave me the thumbs-up and started the video camera.

I took a step around the boulder that we'd used to cover our approach and craned my neck to see the goat. Then I took another more careful step, leaning out toward the drop-off to better see along the ledge. There! For the second time that day, the old billy and I locked eyes. This time he was lying down, and the advantage was decidedly mine.

TEETERING ON THE BRINK

The goat never moved. His head dropped, and for a smoky second it seemed that the 300-grain

Sometimes you have to force a smile on a mountain goat hunt where you'll experience the highest highs and the lowest lows.

Swift bullet had done more than it should ever have been asked to do; he wasn't going over!

For a second only; for then slowly, like the waft of wind from a butterfly's wing that grows to a hurricane, one goat molecule rolled toward the edge. Inexorably, the rest followed, one molecule at a time until the whole goat simply waterfalled over the edge of the drop-off.

I was sickened. Such a magnificent animal's life used up and then wasted in a tumbling, ripping fall down the mountain. In that second, I would have given anything to take the shot back. And then, suddenly, true to the up-and-down definition of a mountain goat hunt, that second passed and the next second turned "down" into "up."

"He's hung up!" Bryan exclaimed.

Jubilation! After the shot, Bryan risked life and limb to visually follow the goat's descent. For 60 yards the dead goat tumbled, destined for thin air, and then miraculously fell into the rocky arms of the one and only snaggly crag that divided the mountainside from 3,000 feet of "nothing but air."

Thank you, Mary.

It took me half-an-hour to work my way down to the eagle aerie cum mountain goat tomb; half-an-hour of adventure that I can only describe as "intensely tentative." While I was at it, the facts

This great August billy goat in British Columbia put the author on the top of the world. Just when everything seems impossible, magic.

of the hunt sank in. Thanks to Bryan Martin's steadfast determination (and to his strong back that carried all my extra gear), and to Harry McCowan for outfitting the hunt, and to Gregg Gutschow for FINALLY taking a mountain goat with his bow and arrow, I'd just taken the mountain goat of a lifetime! An old billy with massive bases and legitimate 10-inch horns!

It was odd, but right then, when I held the beautiful animal in my hands, the definition of mountain goat hunting adapted remarkably and mirrored my feelings. For me, right then, there was no "down" to mountain goat hunting, there was only "up." I'd like to say that the mountain goat hunt ended on this "up" note, but, alas, it did not. As the sun settled behind the nearest mountain to the west, and the trail dimmed, darkened and then disappeared, there was only "down." ∎

Ultimate Big Game Adventures